...ned
...nds,
...vel.

For more than 135 years our
guidebooks have unlocked the secrets
of destinations around the world,
sharing with travellers a wealth of
experience and a passion for travel.

**Rely on Thomas Cook as your
travelling companion on your next trip
and benefit from our unique heritage.**

Thomas Cook **pocket** guides

GOA

Your travelling companion since 1873

Thomas
Cook

Written by Debbie Stowe, updated by Deepti Kapoor

Published by Thomas Cook Publishing
A division of Thomas Cook Tour Operations Limited
Company registration no. 3772199 England
The Thomas Cook Business Park, Unit 9, Coningsby Road,
Peterborough PE3 8SB, United Kingdom
Email: books@thomascook.com, Tel: +44 (0) 1733 416477
www.thomascookpublishing.com

Produced by Cambridge Publishing Management Limited
Burr Elm Court, Main Street, Caldecote CB23 7NU
www.cambridgepm.co.uk

ISBN: 978-1-84848-453-5

© 2007, 2009 Thomas Cook Publishing
This third edition © 2011
Text © Thomas Cook Publishing
Maps © Thomas Cook Publishing/PCGraphics (UK) Limited

Series Editor: Karen Beaulah
Production/DTP: Steven Collins

Printed and bound in Spain by GraphyCems

Cover photography © Simon Reddy/Alamy

CONTENTS

INTRODUCTION 5
Getting to know Goa 8
The best of Goa 10
Symbols key 12

RESORTS 13
Arambol..14
Vagator 20
Anjuna...25
Baga 31
Calangute......................................37
Candolim 44
Morjim, Asvem & Mandrem......48
Panaji...53
Colva..61
Benaulim 66
Palolem 70

EXCURSIONS 75
Bardez taluka 76
Fort Aguada & Sinquerim........78
Dr Salim Ali Bird Sanctuary........81
Old Goa...83
Ponda.............................
Margao..........................

LIFESTYLE 95
Food & drink 96
Menu decoder 100
Shopping 102
Children 105
Sports & activities 107
Festivals & events 109

PRACTICAL INFORMATION...111
Accommodation...........................112
Preparing to go............................114
During your stay 118

INDEX 125

MAPS
Goa 6
Anjuna..24
Baga 30
Calangute 36
Panaji 52
Colva..60
Margao...90

WHAT'S IN YOUR GUIDEBOOK?

Independent authors Impartial, up-to-date information from our travel experts who meticulously source local knowledge.

Experience Thomas Cook's 165 years in the travel industry and guidebook publishing enriches every word with expertise you can trust.

Travel know-how Thomas Cook has thousands of staff working around the globe, all living and breathing travel.

Editors Travel-publishing professionals, pulling everything together to craft a perfect blend of words, pictures, maps and design.

You, the traveller We deliver a practical, no-nonsense approach to information, geared to how you really use it.

● *Fishing boats at Morjim beach*

INTRODUCTION
Getting to know Goa

Getting to know Goa

When you're travelling in Goa, it's sometimes easy to forget that it's just a tiny part of a very big country. The state's sense of identity is so strong that it feels like a nation in its own right, and the area is so lacking in the deprivations and hassles that can occur elsewhere in India that seasoned travellers often refer to it as 'India for beginners'. Its coastline of over 100 km (62 miles) – a good portion of it consisting of golden beaches of a perfection that is rarely encountered outside holiday brochures – is supplemented by a good deal of sites well worth venturing inland for. Goa's decent road and transport network makes it an easy place to get around, whether you choose to do so on the lively local buses that will set you back just a few rupees, in the luxury of a chauffeur-driven car, or – one of the most popular options – by motorbike.

Goa has all the cultural colour of India: if you're after temples, mysticism and Ayurveda, you won't have to look far. But the state also betrays influences from further afield: beautiful churches and villas remain one of the more positive legacies of around 450 years of Portuguese rule. Perhaps the most vibrant subculture in the state grew up through the free spirits who started arriving in the 1960s, when Goa was co-opted on to the hippy trail. In northern resorts such as Arambol and Anjuna, the trail lives on in the hippy stalls, dreadlocks, Bob Marley memorabilia, trance music and a laid-back vibe.

But there's plenty for more active types too. Calangute and Baga have become package hotspots and, with their numerous watersports and pulsating nightlife, it is obvious why. Inland, the administrative capital Panaji also offers a range of options after the sun goes down, with the thumping party boats that cruise up and down the river being among the most popular. Away from the buzz and nightlife are small havens of solitude and relaxation, where you can often have the beach and the sea almost to yourself, and catch a romantic sunset for two. If you get sand fatigue, Goa's backdrop of museums, places of worship, historic sites, animal sanctuaries and spice plantations means that it's impossible to get bored.

Factor in the reasonably cheap prices, welcoming Goans and an abundance of fantastic food – in particular fresh fruit and fish – and you'll start to understand why many wanderers who found their way to Goa never found their way back again.

● *Discover the colour and culture of a world apart*

THE BEST OF GOA

Far more than just a beach resort, Goa has myriad delights to entertain you, from the mystic to the hedonistic. Whether you yearn for the serenity of meditation and massage, or the hair-raising thrills of jet-skiing and parasailing, everything you could ask of a beach holiday is on tap here – and all at an affordable price.

TOP 10 ATTRACTIONS

- **Ayurveda, yoga and meditation** Whether you're a dedicated yogi or just fancy spoiling yourself with a relaxing massage, there are plenty of places where you can be pummelled, stretched or entranced (see page 108).

- **Markets** Visit the thriving local markets, especially Mapusa on a Friday, and mingle in alleyways with locals among the fish, fruit & veg, spice, trinket and sausage sellers, discovering a colourful slice of real Goan life (see page 76).

- **Learn to dive** Discover the amazing marine life around the Goan shore and explore ancient shipwrecks (see page 33).

- **Hidden beaches** You thought all the beaches had been found? Think again. In South Goa, between Benaulim and the state border, discover a string of hidden, undeveloped beaches that still conjure up a vision of paradise (see page 70).

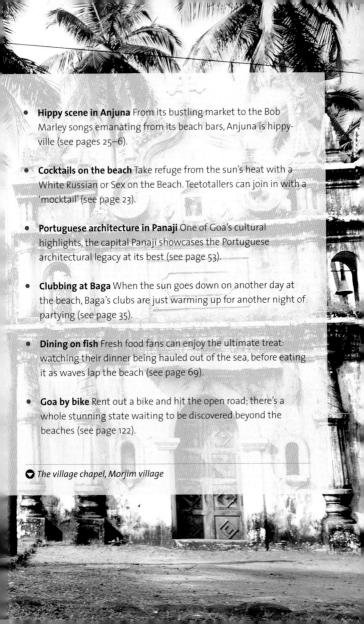

- **Hippy scene in Anjuna** From its bustling market to the Bob Marley songs emanating from its beach bars, Anjuna is hippy-ville (see pages 25–6).

- **Cocktails on the beach** Take refuge from the sun's heat with a White Russian or Sex on the Beach. Teetotallers can join in with a 'mocktail' (see page 23).

- **Portuguese architecture in Panaji** One of Goa's cultural highlights, the capital Panaji showcases the Portuguese architectural legacy at its best (see page 53).

- **Clubbing at Baga** When the sun goes down on another day at the beach, Baga's clubs are just warming up for another night of partying (see page 35).

- **Dining on fish** Fresh food fans can enjoy the ultimate treat: watching their dinner being hauled out of the sea, before eating it as waves lap the beach (see page 69).

- **Goa by bike** Rent out a bike and hit the open road; there's a whole stunning state waiting to be discovered beyond the beaches (see page 122).

The village chapel, Morjim village

SYMBOLS KEY

The following symbols are used throughout this book:

ⓐ address ⓣ telephone ⓕ fax ⓦ website address ⓔ email
ⓞ opening times ❶ important

The following symbols are used on the maps:

ℹ️	information office	○	city
✉️	post office	○	large town
🛍️	shopping	○	small town
🛫	airport	■	point of interest
➕	hospital	══	motorway
🛡️	police station	—	main road
🚌	bus station/stop		minor road
🚆	railway station	—	railway
✝️	church	----	state border
❶	numbers denote featured cafés, restaurants & evening venues

RESTAURANT CATEGORIES
The symbol after the name of each restaurant listed in this guide indicates the cost of a typical three-course meal without drinks for one person:
£ up to 300 rupees ££ 300–600 rupees £££ over 600 rupees

▶ *Goa is a beach lover's dream*

RESORTS
Places under the sun

Arambol

Nestled right up near the northern tip of Goa, sociable Arambol has escaped the influx of package holidaymakers that has been seen by some of the more central beach resorts. Instead, it has been taken over by a different breed: hippies. Independent travellers, free spirits and anyone with natty dreads will fit right in here; in fact it's hard for anyone not to feel at home in a place with such a sense of community. Restaurateurs are friendly and relaxed, there's plenty of communal entertainment like film nights, and dotted around are little notices advertising everything from music lessons to massage. Perhaps as a natural extension of its hippy roots, Arambol is now home to a vibrant yoga and wellness scene that is unmatched anywhere else in the state.

BEACHES

Arambol's beach is still beautiful, with a lingering feeling of how Goa must once have been. Colourful fishing boats pepper the golden sand. To the right as you face out to sea is a rugged hill, with a few palms and cottages. Despite the resort's popularity among the backpacker and hippy crowd, there's always plenty of room on the beach, perhaps because of its relative remoteness. The long and wide expanse of sand holds plenty of eateries, so you'll never be stuck for a spot of lunch or a cooling cocktail. The lush trees dotted among the bars and restaurants mean that the resort feels less commercial than other locations.

You won't have any trouble finding a sunbed and umbrella. As in most of Goa, these are usually owned by the restaurants nearest to them and are typically free to use if you're eating or drinking at that establishment; otherwise you'll be expected to pay a small charge.

If you fancy a dip, be warned that at times the sea can be fairly rough, so weak swimmers may be better off in one of the resort's freshwater lakes.

THINGS TO SEE & DO

Watersports

Fans of peace and quiet will be pleased to hear that Arambol has escaped the noisier, engine-propelled watersports, but adventurous types can do a spot of surfing and paragliding.

Surf Club and Shack Something of a one-stop shop for all your leisure needs, the club not only rents out watersports equipment and gives basic tuition, but also hosts live bands on Tuesday and Friday. Sometimes the bands rehearse all afternoon. There are films on Wednesday and there is an open-deck policy for DJs in the shack in the afternoons and evenings. Other entertainments run the gamut from massage to pool and board games.

🅐 60 m (200 ft) off the south end of Arambol Beach ☏ 98 50 554006
🅔 flyinfishbarbados@hotmail.com

🔺 *Sand, surf and eating shacks at Arambol*

Kite Surf Goa The hours are irregular but, when it's open, you can hire equipment and take surf courses. The best time for kite-surfing is October to April.

ⓐ Next door to Surf Club and Shack

Yoga and meditation

Hippy hub Arambol offers seemingly unlimited ways to treat yourself to a bit of mysticism. Check the noticeboards for new offers. Many outfits spend half the year in Goa and the rest in Dharamsala in north India.

Himalayan Iyengar Yoga Centre One of the most established yoga operators in the area. Five-day courses start every Friday at 08.00. Booking can be done in person every Tuesday at 14.00 from the centre itself.

ⓐ Between Arambol and Mandrem beaches: look for signs

ⓦ www.hiyogacentre.com ⓔ info@hiyogacentre.com ⓛ Mid-Nov–Mar

Panda Tai Chi Meditation and Tai Chi are two of the workshops on offer.

ⓐ Tai Chi Garden next to Priya guesthouse, Coconut Grove and the beach by Full Moon ⓦ www.pandataichi.net ⓔ pandataichi@yahoo.com

ⓛ Nov–mid-Mar

Universal Yoga Daily Ashtanga classes and courses start at 09.00 (except Sunday), while Hatha yoga is from 16.00 to 18.00.

ⓐ Famafa Beach Resort, near Fellini Restaurant ⓣ 94 18 291929

ⓦ www.vijaypoweryoga.com ⓛ Mon–Sat, closed Sun

TAKING A BREAK

Bars & cafés

Arambol essentially consists of one main road leading to the beach, where the majority of eating and drinking options are concentrated. This makes getting lost or failing to find your intended venue practically impossible.

Cookie Wallah £ At the other end of the scale to the health food places, the Cookie Wallah will bring you all manner of guilty indulgences – cakes, cookies, apple pie or chocolate brownies – or a sandwich if you

prefer, while you relax on cushions or low comfy chairs. Very friendly and homely. ❷ Khalchawada, behind Dotcom 🕐 08.00–23.00 or 24.00 daily

Happy Banana Juice Bar £ Fruit fans rejoice! This tiny shack offers juices, shakes, lassis and healthy breakfasts like muesli. Choose from the whole gamut of fruit including mango, papaya, pineapple and pomegranate. Sensation seekers can try out adventurous combinations like the melon and chocolate milkshake. The jolly slogan is: 'Smile a lot. It costs nothing.' ❷ Khalchawada ☎ 99 21 688321 ✉ diya.sanjeev@yahoo.com 🕐 08.00–23.00 daily

Lamuela £ Friendly bistro-café serving freshly made salads, sandwiches, coffee, tea, pure juices, bagels, ice cream, shakes and smoothies, all of which you can enjoy from a swinging seat. It has a small shop, and also offers *reiki*, massage, reflexology, acupuncture, Ayurvedic head and yoga massage, Thai massage, Tai Chi and Chi Gong. A mystic tarot card reader is available on Sunday and Monday. Other options include juggling, acrobatics and fire-juggling classes, and live concerts and jam sessions in the garden. ❷ 292 Khalchawada, around the corner from the church ☎ 98 22 486314 ✉ lamuella@gmail.com 🕐 08.30–23.00 daily (mid-Aug–mid-May)

Double Dutch ££ Large, fun, garden restaurant with trees creating separate sections for a touch of privacy, and a more informal dining area with big cushions to relax on. The Indonesian food gets good write-ups, as do the desserts, which include apple pie, cakes, cheesecake and cookies. Check out what's going on in Arambol on the info board at the entrance, covered in adverts for music lessons, yoga and Ayurveda treatments. There's also a book swap. ❷ Beach Road ☎ 0832 652 5973 ✉ doubledutchgoa@yahoo.co.uk 🕐 07.00–22.00 daily

Magic Park ££ 'Food is energy' is the mantra, and all things vegan abide at Magic Park, a healing, yoga and meditation centre with attached café. The emphasis is on fresh, high-quality produce –

including salads, breads, cakes and juices – in a communal atmosphere.
ⓐ House No 2, Moddlo Waddo ❶ 98 23 619688 ⓔ magicpark@gmx.net
🕑 07.30–22.00 daily

AFTER DARK

Restaurants

Dawat £ Good-humouredly billing itself as the 'budget restaurant for budget people', Dawat offers cheap eats against a background of mellow music. ⓐ Khalchawada ❶ 98 81 463731/284294 🕑 08.00–23.00 daily

Amigo's ££ This Korean restaurant, run by a cool and charming Korean-Ladakhi couple, is a bright and breezy breath of fresh air, and as authentic as you'll get given the circumstances. Go for steaming noodles, kimchi, or the famous meal-in-one-bowl, Bibimbap.
ⓐ Khalchawada ❶ 94 19 178790 ⓔ korean_restaurant@arambol.goa
🕑 09.00–23.00 Mon–Sat, closed Sun

Fellini ££ Highly rated Italian restaurant with an outdoor clay oven from which delectable pizzas emerge after 18.30. Other options include beef, chicken and pasta dishes, or toasties and sandwiches if you just fancy a snack. The relaxed staff and outdoor tables create a laid-back vibe, and there's also a small jewellery shop. ⓐ Beach Road ❶ 97 64 893896
🕑 18.30–23.00 daily (low season); 10.00–23.00 daily (peak season)

Ice and Spice ££ An innocuous-looking set of steps leads down to a large open-air restaurant overlooking paddy fields, where movies are shown on a big screen every night and football every weekend. French and Italian dishes dominate Goan owner Adam Fernandes' menu, while the attached rooms are modern, clean and well priced. ⓐ Beach Road
❶ 98 50 451767 ⓔ fadamisidor@yahoo.com 🕑 08.00–23.00 daily

Loekie Café ££ Another easy-going eatery with cushions and live music. Jam sessions are held on Thursday and Sunday. The menu includes

continental, Italian, Chinese, Indian, English, tandoori, seafood and cocktails. From 09.00 to 20.00 they also offer Ayurvedic massages; to book one, call ① 98 22 037412. ⓐ Beach Road ① 0832 652 9632, 98 22 149097 ② 07.00–23.00 daily

Morning Star ££ Unpretentious eatery, serving a typical beach-shack menu of pizza, European standards, Italian favourites and seafood. ⓐ Harmal Beach ① 98 22 486487 ② 08.00–22.30 daily

Sai Sagar bar and restaurant ££ Rumour has it that Raj, the friendly owner of this place, once appeared on the BBC's *Food & Drink* programme. The Indian food is recommended, and you can sometimes catch a film ⓐ Main Road ① 98 23 836544 ② 07.00–23.00 or later, daily

● *Colourful lanterns on sale in Arambol*

Vagator

Vagator stands at the northern end of the most famous Goan beach strip, with a sudden rugged coastline that's in marked contrast to the touristy sands further south. This more difficult terrain is perhaps fitting because, along with Chapora, Vagator is the last stand of the famous hippy past. In many ways it really does feel like the end of something, where confusingly narrow lanes dotted with ramshackle houses full of *fin-de-siècle* travellers lead down to cliffs and inlets and a rocky sea.

But there's a new Vagator too, visible not only in the coachloads of Indian tourists who come to get an eyeful of hippy flesh, but also in the wonderful restaurants that have opened up around the hilltop, attracting an affluent, modern crowd from Mumbai.

These two worlds continue to coexist peacefully, but the latter knows the former won't last forever, and that the throbbing trance beats will sooner or later become a ghost drifting out of the jungle over the sea.

BEACHES

There are three beaches in the area: from north to south, Vagator, Little Vagator and Ozran. The main one is Vagator, but Little Vagator is also popular with visitors because of the image of the Hindu god Shiva carved into the rocks. As with many Goan resorts, don't be surprised to find yourself sharing the beach with members of the local bovine community.

At the approach to the beach, by the car park, is a small market, where you can enjoy (or endure – they're not to everyone's taste) a freshly made sugar cane juice. There are a few tourist-oriented stalls, but you won't get the hard sell. From the car park, some rough-hewn steps lead down to the beach. Steep and irregular, these are difficult to negotiate and care is required. If you want to swim, it's better to stick to Vagator Beach, which is patrolled by a lifeguard and has a flag-warning system in place; the rocky waters at Ozran make the current unpredictable.

The coastline here has undergone nothing like the commercialisation of the larger resorts. There is the odd place to eat on the beach, but by and large when you're looking out to sea there are cliffs rather than beach shacks behind you. Rocks on the beach and green-brown hills to the right add to the naturalistic, undeveloped feel. Your time here is unlikely to be disturbed by the roar of jet-ski engines: sport in Vagator usually means nothing more energetic than Frisbee® or volleyball.

TAKING A BREAK

Bars & cafés

Bean Me Up £ Lively and popular organic and veggie restaurant, where pizzas, pastas, salads and juices are consumed by a casual crowd in the courtyard. Thursday night is film night; live music or dance is usually on Sunday and there are also Ayurveda treatments available. Children get

● *The natural vibe of Vagator*

mattresses, colouring books and cartoons on the TV. ⓐ 1639/2 Deul Vaddo ⓣ 0832 227 3479 ⓔ beanmeup@usa.net ⓛ 12.00–16.00, 19.00–23.00 Sun–Fri, closed Sat ⓘ Credit cards accepted

Le Bluebird ££ This French-run café and guesthouse enjoys a great reputation, particularly for its seafood. Veggies will also appreciate the wide range of meat-free options. The imported wine and champagne is another big draw. ⓐ Close to Little Vagator Beach ⓣ 0832 227 3695 ⓛ 08.30–17.00 daily

AFTER DARK

Restaurants

Mezcal ££ Goa's been dying for real Mexican food for a long time, and now with Mezcal you might just think you've gone to heaven. Set back in a stylish, solid space, with a mean margarita at the bar, the highlights include tacos, burritos, a whole load of beef options, all kinds of authentic sides and a beautifully spiced rotisserie chicken. ⓐ Hilltop Vagator ⓣ 96 04 800246 ⓦ www.mezcalrestaurantgoa.com ⓛ 11.00–23.00 daily

My Place ££ Traditional Italian food made by the temperamental genius Sarjano. On a good day this place might well do the best gnocchi and ravioli you've ever eaten. But as is often the case with such genius, it can be hit-and-miss. ⓐ Near petrol pumps ⓣ 09 76 702 0138 ⓛ 11.00–23.00 daily

Sakana ££ Cool, authentic and unpretentious, this Japanese restaurant serves sushi and sashimi along with more hearty dishes such as yakitori and beef and onion gyudon. All are made using the highest-quality imported ingredients. Sake is also available. ⓐ Chapora Road, near petrol pumps ⓣ 98 90 135502 ⓛ 13.00–23.00 daily

Thalassa ££ Greek taverna food done properly, in a spectacular hilltop location. Thalassa has been one of the resounding hits of the last few

seasons, gaining rave reviews and drawing a dedicated following from the Mumbai crowd – a following that's now been reflected in its rising prices. ⓐ Little Vagator hilltop ① 98 50 033537 ⓦ www.myspace.com/thalassagoa ① 16.00–24.00 daily

Willy's ££ The staff and food both get good reviews in this restaurant, which has the usual pizzas, sandwiches, continental, Indian and Chinese fare. Follow it with ice cream and cocktails. ⓐ Vagator Beach Road ① 0832 227 3566 ⓔ willy100@hotmail.com ① 08.00–23.00 daily

⬤ *Rugged rocks at Vagator beach*

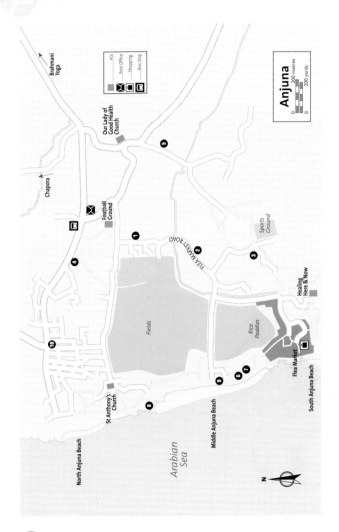

Anjuna

Brahmani Yoga

Chapora

Our Lady of Good Health Church

POI
Post Office
Shopping
Bus Stop

Football Ground

Sports Ground

FLEA MARKET ROAD

Healing Here & Now

Fields

Rice Paddies

Flea Market

St Anthony's Church

North Anjuna Beach

Middle Anjuna Beach

South Anjuna Beach

Arabian Sea

N

0   200 metres
0   200 yards

Anjuna

Anjuna will appeal to anyone who finds its moniker, 'freak capital of the world', a good thing, and vies with Arambol, further up the coast, for the title of Goa's top hippy resort. It's more spread out than Arambol and as a result lacks some of the community feel, but the renowned Wednesday flea market floods the town with atmosphere and character. Anjuna was once famous for trance parties; now the authorities are clamping down on noise pollution, and such gatherings are becoming harder to find. But you can still have a great night out here, particularly on market day, which draws in visitors from all around. Taxi drivers are usually the best information sources on parties.

BEACHES

Even on market day, the beach at Anjuna remains fairly free of crowds. It's a wide, flat expanse of sand, dotted with a few beach shacks with a smattering of tables on the sand and market stalls, but is nowhere near as cluttered as the more package-oriented resorts further south. The beach is spacious with tall palms, and the unusual black rock formation is perfectly in keeping with the alternative feel of the resort. You don't get as many swimmers as elsewhere, but the water is relatively safe. Sunbeds are also available.

Primarily a market town, Anjuna does attract more than its fair share of seasoned hawkers, and these spill over on to the beach. They can be fairly determined, but if your 'noes' are firm enough they should leave you alone. More welcome beach entrepreneurs are the jugglers and fire-eaters who sometimes strut their stuff in the early evening.

THINGS TO SEE & DO

Flea Market
One of Goa's top tourist draws, the huge Anjuna flea market is an overwhelming fusion of all the colour, noise and commerce of Goa. If you

don't find something you want to buy from the shoes, clothes, jewellery, music, pashminas, shawls, cushion covers, CDs, spices, bric-a-brac, hookah pipes, sunglasses and cigarettes on offer, you must be very hard to please. Part of the appeal is that the market attracts many vibrant individuals, from expat hippies to Goan matriarchs and Indian men with piercings that seem to defy science. Not everyone exudes a positive presence, though: some of the traders and beggars can be persistent to the point of annoying. If it's getting tiresome, head for the covered jewellery market run by Tibetan vendors, where you'll get less of the hard sell. You can also appease your conscience at the section for project and charity appeals. There are several cafés, most quite far from the entrance, plus ice-cream *wallahs* doing the rounds.

ⓐ Market Road, at southern end of beach ⓒ 08.00–17.00 Wed (Oct–Apr)

Yoga & wellness

Healing Here & Now A variety of therapeutic and detox treatments are on offer, including colonic cleanses and ozone therapy.

ⓐ Behind Xavier's restaurant ⓣ 0832 226 8158/0832 227 3487
ⓦ www.healinghereandnow.com ⓔ info@healinghereandnow.com

⬤ *Surf and sailpower at Anjuna beach*

● *Anjuna market is a big attraction*

Brahmani Yoga All types of yoga are catered for at Brahmani, a popular studio run by experienced instructor Julie Martin. Their teacher-training programme is well known for its rigour and discipline, but the biggest virtue of the centre, which is set in the grounds of an old Portuguese villa, is how they welcome absolute beginners with open arms.
ⓐ Hotel Bougainvillea ❶ 93 70 568639 ⓦ www.brahmaniyoga.com
🕐 07.30–18.30 daily

TAKING A BREAK

Bars & cafés
Artjuna £ ❶ Initially a handicrafts and lifestyle space where owner Moshe handed out free drinks to tired husbands, the café that's grown up here over the years has now become the main draw. The coffee is arguably the best in Goa, and the grilled sandwiches and salads, while nothing fancy, aren't that far behind. The attached children's play area and yoga shala add to the happy air, as do the prices. ⓐ 972 Monteiro Vaddo ❶ 0832 227 4794 ⓦ www.artjuna.com 🕐 09.30–21.30 daily

Café Diogo £ ❷ A charming Goan-run, hippy-oriented affair, the one-room Café Diogo is an Anjuna institution. They serve up a legendary toasted avocado sandwich, fresh fruit juices and lassis and lots of backpacker staples – like the wonderful banana pancake – that are fast fading elsewhere. ⓐ Flea Market Road ⓛ 08.30–17.30 daily

German Bakery £ ❸ This is the original bakery that has spawned imitators all over India. Its juices, sweets and coffee are particularly recommended, and it also serves main courses. ⓐ Behind the flea market near the sports ground ⓣ 90 96 058775 ⓛ 08.30–23.00 daily

AFTER DARK

Restaurants
Blue Tao Restaurant & Pizzeria ££ ❹ Highly rated health food restaurant serving vegetarian, vegan and organic dishes, home-made ice cream and genuine Italian pizzas from the wood oven. ⓐ 300 m

△ *Hard at work in the kitchen at Om Made Café*

(330 yds) west of post office ☎ 89 75 061435 ✉ bluetao@rocketmail.com ⏰ 09.00–23.00 daily

The Jam Connection ££ ➎   The place to fix the munchies, The Jam Connection has been a fixture of the Anjuna scene for years now. Decadent cocoa drinks, chocolate-smothered desserts and Austrian coffee combine with salads, juices and hummus to create the perfect balance between health and sin. ⓐ A1 Friend's Corner, near Orchard Stores ☎ 98 22 118616 ⏰ 11.00–23.00 Sun–Fri, closed Sat

Janet and John's Multicuisine Restaurant ££ ➏   Friendly place offering a 35-dish seafood buffet on Mondays. ⓐ Anjuna Beach, 300 m (330 yds) from the flea market ☎ 0832 229 3713 ⏰ 08.00–24.00 daily

Lilliput ££ ➐   Facing out to sea, this charming bar and restaurant enjoys mellow music and a pool table. ⓐ Govenkar Vaddo, Anjuna Beach ☎ 98 22 132479 🌐 www.cafelilliput.com ⏰ 08.00–24.00 daily

Om Made Café ££ ➑   Standing whitewashed and chic amid the tired joints of Anjuna beach, Om Made is the evolution of the beach-shack made flesh. French chef Gregory brings sophistication and class to the menu, with items such as Masala Chai Frappé, Kokum Iced Tea and Raw Papaya Salad. ⓐ Prais de San Anton, North Anjuna Beach 🌐 www.ommadecafe.com ⏰ 09.00–19.00 daily

Shore Bar ££ ➒   Converted from the excesses of its raver heyday into a more relaxed beachfront hangout, Shore Bar draws the customers in with a cool atmosphere, wide selection of dependable food and drink and a bunch of smart, happy staff. Essentially, it's the king of the beach shacks. ⓐ Middle Anjuna Beach ☎ 09 82 238 3795 ⏰ 07.00–24.00 daily

Starco ££ ➓   Loud and lively bar and restaurant serving Indian and continental food. Sit outside if you can, to enjoy the fairy lights. ⓐ At the Starco junction ⏰ 08.30–24.00 daily

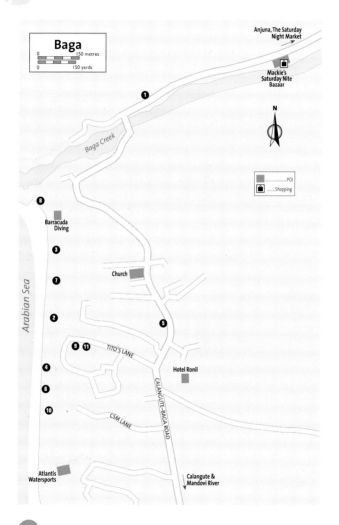

Baga

0   150 metres
0   150 yards

Anjuna, The Saturday
Night Market

Mackie's
Saturday Nite
Bazaar

N

Baga Creek

POI
Shopping

Barracuda
Diving

Church

Arabian Sea

TITO'S LANE

Hotel Ronil

CALANGUTE–BAGA ROAD

CSM LANE

Atlantis
Watersports

Calangute &
Mandovi River

Baga

Probably Goa's nightlife capital, Baga is home to the big-name clubs that attract the party set, and its after-dark scene is considered more sophisticated than nearby Calangute's. Here, nights are for partying hard; days are for recovering and going for it again, this time on watersports such as jet-skis or parasailing. One of the main package-tour hubs, the resort is full of Europeans flown in by tour companies, so it attracts groups of friends out to socialise and have fun with other holidaymakers. Because of the youthful vibe, there are a lot of watersports options, with operators patrolling the beach looking for customers. As well as the extreme stuff, you also have the more sedate options of crocodile- and dolphin-spotting on the Mandovi River: the crocodiles nestle among the tree-lined riverbanks and the dolphins cavort where the river meets the sea.

As well as the sea there is the Baga River, which meets the sea north of the beach and is a good option for weaker swimmers who find the sea waves offputting.

BEACHES

Crescent-shaped Baga beach is slightly less crowded and developed than its immediate neighbour, Calangute. At low tide the beach is wide and gently sloping, but at high tide it does get fairly narrow. You shouldn't have trouble in finding a sunbed – as usual these are free if you're eating in the restaurant that owns them, otherwise a charge of around 50 rupees is normal.

The sea is calmer than at Calangute, so relatively safe for swimming, but serious surfers will have to go elsewhere for their waves. Along with the watersports wallahs, masseurs also wander the beach selling their services. But there's no need to do anything on Baga Beach: with the paddy fields behind you, verdant cliffs to your left and waves crashing rhythmically off the rocks, it's enough simply to relax and take in the scenery.

◆ *Beautiful Baga*

THINGS TO SEE & DO

Markets
The Saturday Night Market The larger of the two Baga markets, this lovely night-time bazaar has clothes, crafts and jewellery along with live music and fire-twirling.

ⓐ Arpora, halfway between Baga and Anjuna ⓛ 16.30–24.00 Sat (Nov–Mar)

Mackie's Saturday Nite Bazaar Smaller and calmer than the rival Saturday Night Market further out of town (see above), this bazaar is within walking distance of Baga.

ⓐ Close to Marinha Dourada, near Baga Creek ⓣ 98 81 772990
ⓛ 18.00–24.00 Sat (Nov–Mar)

Watersports
Atlantis Watersports Offers scuba diving, jet-skiing, parasailing and windsurfing at negotiable prices.

ⓐ Near Hotel Villa, Goesa Baga ⓣ 98 90 047272

Barracuda Diving PADI scuba diving courses and snorkelling and a pool for learners.

ⓐ Sun Village Resort, Arpora Village ⓣ 0832 227 9409/98 22 182402
ⓦ www.barracudadiving.com ⓔ info@barracuda.com
ⓛ 08.00–14.00 daily

TAKING A BREAK

Cafés
Lila Café ££ ❶ Salads, rolls and omelettes are on offer at this popular German-run bakery and café. You can also enjoy some tasty cakes and desserts. ⓐ Baga Creek ⓣ 0832 227 9843 ⓦ www.lilacafegoa.com
ⓔ lilacafe@sify.com ⓛ 09.00–18.00 Wed–Mon (Oct–Apr), closed Tues

AFTER DARK

Restaurants

Le Marin beach shack £ **❷** One of many similar options on Baga beach, this is a good place for couples with two-seater tables facing out to the sea. The service is efficient, and there's often sport showing on the TV. **ⓐ** Near Tito's, Sauntavaddo **❶** 98 22 877718 **🕓** 08.00–23.00 daily

Andrew's ££ **❸** Quiet, calm and cool, this beach shack has a thatched roof, swing seats, plants and a pool table. **ⓐ** 7/62 Sauntavaddo **❶** 98 22 151678 **🕓** 07.30–last customer, daily

Antonio's ££ **❹** One of the first shacks to set up on the beach, affable Antonio's has a nice atmosphere, great food and friendly staff. It's a quiet place, where you can relax among the plants and peruse the magazine collection. There's a brightly painted mural and the obligatory Bob Marley artwork. Sunday night's seafood barbecue serves up kingfish, shark, tuna and rockfish fillet. **ⓐ** Cobravaddo, Baga Beach **❶** 0832 228 2108 **🕓** 09.00–23.30 or 24.00 daily

Casa Portuguesa ££ **❺** Housed in an exquisite Goan-Portuguese manor replete with antiques and a stylish terrace, the cuisine includes indulgent specials such as roast wild boar. **ⓐ** On the left-hand side of Baga Road, 200 m (220 yds) past the Hotel Ronil **❶** 0832 227 7024 **🌐** www.casa-portuguesa-goa.com **🕓** 19.00–23.00 Tues–Sun, closed Mon (Nov–Apr)

TGI Friday ££ **❻** This shack is as relaxed and lively as the restaurant chain whose name it is cheekily borrowing. **ⓐ** Near Tito's, to the left of Antonio's facing the sea **❶** 98 221 39660 **🕓** 08.00–24.00 or until last customer leaves, daily

Zanzibar ££ **❼** With leather seats and an upmarket ambience, this is a more sophisticated alternative to most of its competitors. You can also

pick up a pair of flip-flops here. ⓐ Down Tito's Lane and to right, on beach by volleyball net ❶ 98 23 274707 ⓛ 09.00–24.00 daily

Bars & clubs

Britto's ££ ❽   Baga stalwart with highly rated seafood plus a range of Indian and continental choices, Britto's also has a reputation as a lively nightspot. Its popularity means at peak times it can take a while to get served – but you can enjoy the view while you wait. The cakes and pastries are top-notch as well. ⓐ Baga Beach ❶ 0832 227 7331
ⓛ 07.00–03.00 daily, closed 21 June–10 Aug

Café Mambo ££ ❾   Affiliated to and just closer to the sea than Tito's, this beachfront venue is not quite as lively as its mother club, but is still one of the top nightspots in the area, playing host to big international DJs. Dinner is served from 19.00, and the club starts at 22.00.
ⓐ On beachfront, Tito's Lane ❶ 0832 227 9895 ⓛ 24 hours daily
ⓘ Admission charge for disco

Chasing Chengs ££ ❿   Relaxing hangout with cushions around the tables and an extensive cocktail menu. On Thursday there's a barbecue with a Brazilian dancer in attendance, while Saturday is firework night, all from 21.00. ⓐ Baga Beach ❶ 98 81 475746 ⓛ 10.00–24.00 daily

Tito's £££ ⓫   Now over 35 years old, this legendary Baga nightclub has hosted Richard Gere and the cream of the Bollywood set among other beautiful people. The restaurant serves Goan cuisine, pizzas and home-made desserts, and there's also an outdoor pub. Entertainment runs the gamut from magicians to Goan folk dancing, while club nights include jungle, retro, karaoke and hip hop, plus ladies' night. ⓐ Tito's Lane
❶ 0832 227 9895 ⓦ www.titos.in ⓛ Disco from 22.30–04.00 daily
ⓘ Admission charge for men and couples

Calangute

Arabian Sea

Baga & Anjuna

POI
Post Office
Shopping
Bus Stop

CALANGUTE–BAGA ROAD

Our Lady of Piety Chapel

Calangute Market

CALANGUTE–ANJUNA ROAD

Ayurvedic Natural Health Centre

St Anthony's Chapel

CHOGM ROAD

N

HOLIDAY STREET

Kerkar Art Complex

Day Tripper Tours and Travel

Literati Bookshop and Café

Calangute

Calangute was the first Goan resort that foreigners homed in on. It has never looked back and is now the most popular holiday destination in the state. The name means 'land of the fisherman', but it's abundantly clear that it's tourism rather than fishing that is now the town's main concern. It was the hippies who first happened upon the resort and got the tourism ball rolling, but Calangute is now decidedly mainstream: while you can still pick up hippy clothes, bags and knick-knacks from the stalls, the alternative travellers now go to Arambol and Anjuna. These days, Calangute is a veritable temple to tourism, with wall-to-wall beach shacks, top entertainment and eating options and Western-style shopping facilities. All of this attracts plenty of Indians as well as overseas visitors, all enjoying the holiday vibe.

The crowd consists of holidaymakers who prefer to have everything they could possibly need at their fingertips and don't want to work too hard to get it. With so many different ways to pass the time, from just messing about on the beach and playing a spot of volleyball to hair-raising watersports and teeming nightspots, there's something for everyone, which makes Calangute a good choice for family groups, or gangs of pals looking to party hard at night and sleep it off on the beach the next day.

Despite its package 'n' party reputation, Calangute yields some surprisingly cultural treats. It's one of the best beach resorts in the state for art lovers, with several galleries of note, many of which also offer works for sale. Shopaholics will also have their appetites sated in the town, which has both posh designer boutiques and an Indian market.

BEACHES

The central and busiest area of the beach is at the end of the road leading to the roundabout, where a set of wide steps leads down to the sand. Here you'll find a selection of stalls and shops. Despite Calangute's popularity, it is possible to get away from the sunbathing masses. The

beach is very wide, and there's space both in front of and behind the rows of sunbathers. While the main section is heaving with sunbeds and umbrellas, if you're prepared to walk a little way either north or south you'll come to less populated parts where you can find some privacy and see some empty sand among the sun-seekers. Those wanting a more active time are also well catered for in Calangute, with watersports

◆ *You'll still find peaceful spots in popular Calangute*

hawkers constantly strolling around the beach aiming to put tourists in boats, in the air or on jet-skis. There are also volleyball nets if you don't want your activity too strenuous, although in the Goan heat almost any activity can feel a bit much. Cooling off in the water is always tempting, and usually safe, but it can get rough, especially in the afternoon. Look out for a lifeguard before you venture out.

THINGS TO SEE & DO

Ayurveda
Ayurvedic Natural Health Centre All sorts of yoga and Ayurvedic treatments, from one-off email consultations and two-and-a-half-hour taster programmes to six-week intensive yoga courses for all abilities. Helpful staff offer free guided tours, 10.30–17.30 Mon–Sat, closed Sun. ⓐ Chogm Road, Saligao ⓣ 0832 240 9036/94 22 448973 ⓦ www.health andayurveda.com ⓔ info@healthandayurveda.com ⓛ 10.00–20.30 daily

Calangute Market
In a congested part of town, the market is another good opportunity to hone your haggling skills, whether you're after leather goods, clothes, jewellery souvenirs, metalwork or some food. Slightly further towards the beach, by the church, you can pick up Tibetan and Kashmiri textiles and handicrafts, and even further on there are sarongs, other beach essentials and fortune-tellers. While you're there, pop into the eye-catching temple.
ⓐ Town centre ⓛ Roughly 09.00–19.00 daily

Kerkar Art Complex
Hosting the sculptures and paintings of the founder, famous Goan watercolourist Subodh Kerkar, plus other Indian artists. The site also has an open-air auditorium, the venue for concerts of classical Indian music and dance on Tuesdays between 18.45 and 20.30.
ⓐ Gaura Vaddo, South Calangute ⓣ 0832 227 6017 ⓦ www.subodh kerkar.com ⓔ subodhkerkar@satyam.net.in

Literati Bookshop and Café For the range of quality fiction on offer, Literati is one of the best bookshops not only in Goa but in India as a whole. Add to that a strong non-fiction section, an admirable lack of self-help and business books, comfortable sofas and great coffee and you'll find yourself browsing the shelves here for a very long time.
ⓐ E/1-282 Gaura Vaddo ⓣ 0832 227 7740 Ⓦ www.literati-goa.com
Ⓛ 10.00–18.30 Mon–Sat, closed Sun

Watersports & boat trips

Calangute and Baga are the epicentre of Goa's watersports industry, with windsurfing, jet-skiing and parasailing just a few of the options. Calangute is also a good starting point for exploring further afield.

Day Tripper Tours and Travel The usual tours and boat trips are on offer within Goa plus trips over several days further afield to the Taj Mahal and Golden Triangle.

🔺 *Parasailing is one sporting option*

ⓐ E1/79A Gaura Vaddo, near Kamat Complex ⓣ 0832 227 6726
ⓦ www.daytrippergoa.com ⓔ info@daytrippergoa.com ⓛ 09.00–17.30
Mon–Sat, 09.00–12.30 Sun

TAKING A BREAK

Bars & cafés
Infantaria Pastry Shop £ ❶ Popular bakery with pastries, cakes,
croissants and snacks also available to take away. The noticeboard is a
great source of information on yoga and Ayurveda in the area.
ⓐ Unta Waddo ⓣ 0832 329 1290 ⓛ 07.30–24.00 daily

Baba au Rhum ££ ❷ A French-run café and bakery that models itself
on the Parisian neighbourhood hangout and succeeds, with an added
hippy vibe of course. The fresh pastries are second to none and the ham
and cheese baguette (with ham from a local expat English butchers) is
rightly famous. Then there's the coffee, fresh fruit sorbets and chocolate
eclairs... ⓐ 450 Cuddos Vaddo, Arpora ⓣ 98 22 078759 ⓛ 08.30–16.00,
19.00–22.30 Mon–Sat, closed Sun

AFTER DARK

Restaurants
Florentine's £ ❸ One of the most famous restaurants in Goa, its
renown comes from one dish alone: the chicken cafreal. Lightly fried
after spending many hours marinating in a mixture of garlic, chilli,
coriander and secret spices, the dish is present at virtually every table,
and though other items can satisfy, it's only really about one thing.
ⓐ Chogm Road, Saligao ⓣ 0832 227 8122 ⓛ 11.30–15.00, 18.30–22.30
Tues–Sun, closed Mon

The Indian Kitchen £ ❹ Exclusively vegetarian food and drinks are
served in this popular Indian restaurant, which draws a returning Indian
and European clientele for good service and buzzing atmosphere. The

menu includes Goan specialities too. ⓐ Behind Our Lady of Piety Chapel, Calangute–Baga Road ⓣ 0832 227 7555 ⓛ 18.00–23.00 daily (Nov–Apr)

Horizon ££ ❺ Serving mainly Chinese and Indian food – the prawn biryani is particularly recommended. Live football is shown on the TV and there's also a pool table. ⓐ Unta Waddo ⓣ 98 22 484114 ⓛ 08.00–last customer daily

Midaas Touch ££ ❻ From the outside, this gaudy place resembles a water park. Inside it's bright and cheerful, with good-quality Goan, Chinese and continental food, sometimes accompanied by live music. The air-conditioned dining room offers much-needed respite from the heat. ⓐ Calangute–Anjuna Road, opposite Benetton ⓣ 0832 228 2808 ⓔ midaastouch2003@yahoo.com ⓛ 11.00–24.00 daily

ⓐ *Relax and fill up at Travel Bar*

Souza Lobo ££ ❼ A grand dame of the Calangute scene, this place is over 80 years old. There's live music on Wednesday and Sunday, and it fills up quickly over the weekend. The salads, steaks and seafood are particularly recommended. ⓐ On the beach, Central Calangute ❶ 0832 228 1234/227 6463 ⓦ www.souzalobo.com ⓔ jude@souzalobo.com ⓛ 11.00–23.00 daily

Tibetan Kitchen ££ ❽ With an excellent reputation built up over 20 years, the Tibetan Kitchen is relaxed and atmospheric, serving big portions of good-value food. Magazines and board games are available, with last orders at 23.00. ⓐ Set back in an alleyway off Beach Road, close to the beach ❶ 0832 227 5744/99 22 590898 ⓔ thetibkit@yahoo.com ⓛ 17.00–24.00 daily (Oct–Apr)

Waves ££ ❾ Set in the Kerkar Art Complex, this place gives the usual Goan and Indian staples an artistic twist. As you'd expect, the place is designed with care and style that will delight anyone with beach-shack fatigue. ⓐ Gaura Vaddo, South Calangute ❶ 0832 227 6017 ⓦ www.subodhkerkar.com ⓔ subodhkerkar@satyam.net.in

The Copper Bowl £££ ❿ Away from the crowds in the backstreets of Calangute, this restaurant at the luxury Pousada Touma resort serves exceptionally fine Goan cuisine of both Hindu and Portuguese varieties, without drowning them in the usually attendant oil. The resulting dishes are incredibly light yet packed with raw flavours. ⓐ Pousada Touma, Porba Vaddo ❶ 0832 227 9061 ⓛ 07.30–22.30 daily

Travel Bar £££ ⓫ Run by Angeline Lobo, an extremely resourceful young Goan lady who also has a great travel agency on site, this bar and restaurant – a favourite of British expats – boasts a secluded courtyard with big wooden tables, a well-stocked bar and a solid menu of salads, meats and seafood. Open throughout the monsoon, and offers Wi-Fi. ⓐ Opposite Tarcar Ice Factory, Calangute main road ❶ 0832 227 5788/98 50 471639 ⓛ 09.00–16.00, 19.00–23.00 daily

Candolim

Just south of Baga and Calangute, Candolim is placed well enough to have developed a decent tourist infrastructure, but removed enough to have retained some peace, quiet and privacy. This makes it a good choice for anyone who's more likely to be up at seven in the morning because the beach is empty at that time, rather than because they're staggering home from a nightclub. While there are watersports to enjoy if you wish, the main hubs for high-octane thrills in the surf are Baga and Calangute to the north and Sinquerim to the south, which leaves Candolim relatively free from the roar of jet-ski motors and shrieks of air-bound tourists.

If you've had your fill of English breakfasts and fancy some genuine Goan fare, there are some authentic eateries among the tourist traps. The decent selection of restaurants appeals to slightly older holidaymakers who are no longer watching every penny, and prices are a little higher here than in some comparable resorts. Candolim is also home to some posh designer boutiques that are a world away from the cheap and cheerful hippy stalls in Arambol or Anjuna.

BEACHES

Compared to Calangute and Baga to the north, the beach at Candolim will seem refreshingly crowd-free. Long and straight, lined by sand dunes and palm trees, it has the postcard perfection common to Goa's prettier resorts. It also has fewer beach shacks, which means that between the restaurants and their plentiful sunbeds you can find empty tracts of sand, perfect to lie down on if you're seeking a bit of solitude. You will need your towel though – the sand can get scorching as the day progresses. If you arrive and find you've forgotten a beach essential, there's a small market on the approach road. You will sometimes find a lifeguard on duty, but it cannot be guaranteed and, while swimming is mostly safe, the sea can get rough at times.

THINGS TO SEE & DO

Meditation and yoga
Tao Zen
Iyengar-style yoga classes at 08.00 from Monday to Friday and
meditation at 16.30 Monday to Friday. Classes take place on a sea-facing
roof terrace.
ⓐ Thomson Villa, near English Rose, Candolim Beach Road
ⓣ 96 04 636437 ⓦ www.ramayoga.com ⓔ info@ramayoga.com

⬤ *Meeting the locals on Candolim beach*

Trips
John's Boat Tours
Up and running for 14 years, John's offers dolphin and crocodile trips, fishing, snorkelling at Grand Island, plus trips to the Anjuna flea market and spice plantation, which often include a barbecue or free drinks.
ⓐ Candolim Beach Road ⓣ 0832 652 0190

TAKING A BREAK

Bars & cafés
Café Chocolatti £ Indulge your sweet tooth at this family-run temple to chocolate, where cakes are baked on site. Paninis and salads are also available. ⓐ 409 Fort Aguada Road, opposite State Bank of India
ⓣ 0832 247 9340, 93 26 112006 ⓔ rrebelo@sancharnet.in ⓛ 10.00–19.00 Mon–Sat, closed Sun

Calamari £ Twinings tea is a highlight at this pleasant beach shack, where you can also rent a towel if you need one. ⓐ Dando Beach, close to Santana Beach Resort ⓣ 0832 329 0506/93 26 102242
ⓛ 08.00–23.00 daily

AFTER DARK

Restaurants
King Cane Fast Food £ Home-cooked Goan treats with a turnover so high it's safe for the Western stomach, this street-cart near the Candolim veg market is a legend among the locals. Husband-and-wife team Salvador and Maria serve the best beef-chilli-fry around, with roast beef sandwiches and chicken drumsticks among other delights. To find them just look for the crowd. ⓐ Ordo Candolim, behind veg market ⓣ 98 23 464142 ⓛ 17.30–21.30 Mon–Sat, closed Sun

Claudina's Beach Shack ££ This place is distinguished by a few comfy chairs that seem to belong in a grandmother's sitting room rather than a

beach shack and a bookshop. ❸ First shack to the left of beach on approach road ❶ 98 22 158441 ❺ 09.00–23.00 daily

Inferno ££ The inferno theme touches both the décor and the food, with flaming sizzlers a restaurant highlight. Incongruously, Inferno is no-smoking inside, but those who want to light up can do so outside. Both the seafood and service are good. ❸ Murrod Vaddo, Candolim Beach Road ❶ 0832 227 6250/98 22 140130 ❺ 09.30–23.30 daily

Spotty's ££ Loud, lively and friendly, Spotty's has a swing seat, a pool table and a long cocktail list. Thursday is barbecue night from 19.00, and you can also hire bikes and book boat trips here. ❸ On the beach ❶ 98 22 144833 ❺ 08.00–01.00 daily

Sunny Side Up ££ A slightly more upmarket beach shack that's owned and run by Delhiites, the North Indian food on offer – especially the tandoori chicken – is superb. Western and Goan dishes are of a good standard too, and there's a wide range of cocktails. ❸ 360° Beach Resort, Candolim Beach ❶ 0832 645 3971 ❺ 08.30–23.00 daily

Teama ££ This rooftop restaurant serves up Goan, Indian, Chinese, continental and seafood, with live music on Tuesday, Friday and Sunday from 19.30 onwards, while the pub below fills the gaps with karaoke on Monday and Thursday. ❸ Murrod Vaddo, near Candolim Beach car park ❶ 0832 248 9774 ❿ www.teamagoa.com ❺ 08.30–24.00 daily

Clubs
Club Fresh £££ Where the chi-chi Delhi and Mumbai set likes to party (along with the Russians), Club Fresh serves up a range of international and domestic DJs to go with an extensive and expensive food and drinks menu. If you're into wearing white with your shades on at night then this is definitely the place for you. ❸ Murrod Vaddo, opposite Silver Sands Resort ❶ 90 11 611450 ❿ www.clubfreshgoa.com ❺ 18.00–22.00 Tues–Sun, closed Mon

Morjim, Asvem & Mandrem

Stretching for 10 km (6 miles) between the Siolim River and Arambol, the connected beaches of Asvem, Morjim and Mandrem have until the last five or so years been largely ignored by tourism. That's all changing now though, with this area seen by many as the future of north Goa.

It's difficult to pinpoint an exact feel – boutique resorts and ultra-cool restaurants slip quietly into Russian villages and sleepy hippy enclaves, before turning into luxury yoga retreats and resorts again – yet the overriding impression is one of peace, calm and sophistication, with none of the aggressive development of Bardez further south. Part of the reason for this is the geography: these villages are very much spread out, with no discernible centre to the area. Another factor is the type of tourist who generally winds up here, with a higher proportion of older, wealthier Europeans than anywhere else. Morjim is a slight exception, with an often negative reputation as a Russian ghetto (its nickname is "Little Moscow"), but even here the vibe is still open and inclusive. The region is also becoming popular with educated and wealthy Indian travellers, with many opening cafés and restaurants here too. Prices in the area are generally higher than in the rest of Goa.

Away from the beaches, the towns and villages are more Hindu than elsewhere in Goa, and although modern in an Indian sense are still relatively untouched by 21st-century tourism.

BEACHES

The three resorts form one long beach, broken up by rivers, sandbanks and creeks, quite often blissfully devoid of people and always full of natural beauty. At low tide the sands seem to stretch out forever, full of wading birds and groups of fishermen hauling in their nets. A great deal of wildlife can be found on the mudflats and rugged dunes at the southern end of Morjim, where the beach meets the Siolim River. Further north, as it turns into Asvem and then Mandrem, the sands become softer and more obviously beautiful. Along this coast you're just as likely

to see pines as palm trees, with their stark silhouettes lending a different kind of mood and a drama all of their own.

THINGS TO SEE & DO

Sushumna Yoga and Pilates

Set in the grounds of the plush and spacious Aquatica complex, Sushumna is run by a group of highly experienced teachers who combine both yoga and pilates in classes for all levels of students. Weekly passes are available, as are daily drop-ins. The attached restaurant has a special menu designed to cater to Sushumna's students.

ⓐ Aquatica Resort, Morjim–Asvem road ① 99 23 219254 Ⓦ www. sushumna.in ⓔ info@sushumna.in ① 08.00–19.00 daily

🔺 *Cross draped in flowers at Morjim beach*

Banyan Tree

Away from the Mandrem beach in the village of Dandos Wadda, this ancient Banyan tree sprawls out beside the nearby river, its vast canopy of alien-like tendrils rising into the air before diving back into the ground so that it's impossible to tell where the roots end and the branches begin.

ⓐ Dandos Wadda; turn right after the Mandrem temple then left at the small bridge in the fields

TAKING A BREAK

Bars and cafés

Café Nu ££ A sister venture to the Saligao-based Sublime restaurant, this café and bar serves gourmet snack food in a laid-back and unpretentious setting surrounded by palms off the back of the main Mandrem road. Light and tasty treats like pomegranate, chicken and rucola salad vie for place with hot dishes such as banana-wrapped steamed fillet of fish and open-face lasagne. ⓐ House No 182, opposite O Saiba Guesthouse, Junas Waddo ⓣ 98 50 658568 ⓛ 10.00–15.00, 18.00–22.00 daily

🔺 *The colourful entrance of La Plage restaurant in Asvem*

AFTER DARK

Restaurants

By The Bay ££ This restaurant offers a solid and spicy selection of Goan dishes – including a fantastically smoky Sausage Chilli Fry – as well as good Chinese, continental and seafood options. ⓐ Montego Bay Beach Village, Vithaldas Waddo ⓣ 98 22 150847 ⓛ 08.00–24.00 daily

Miaou Miaou Restaurant @ Villa River Cat ££ Something of an oddity, the Villa River Cat is a hotel that seems more akin to an eccentric home. Whatever it is, it's wonderful, and the attached restaurant is wonderful too. ⓐ Villa River Cat, 438/1 Junas Waddo ⓣ 0832 224 7928/98 23 610001 ⓔ miaoumiaouresto@gmail.com ⓛ 18.30–23.30 Sun–Fri, closed Sat

Aquatica £££ This restaurant merges fresh ingredients, health-consciousness and French technique to great effect. Don't be fooled by the health aspect though: there are flavoursome meat, fish and veg options aplenty – and some potent cocktails too. ⓐ Morjim–Asvem road ⓦ www.aquaticagoa.in ⓛ 09.00–22.30 daily

La Plage £££ Appearing like a white mirage on the sands, this famous French beachfront restaurant has been a destination in itself for years now. ⓐ Asvem Beach ⓣ 98 22 121712 ⓛ 08.30–22.00 daily

Bars and clubs

Marbela Beach £££ Modelling itself as an 'Ibiza-style' venue, this lounge bar, restaurant and resort includes wooden decking, white-on-white colour scheme and VIP sofas. ⓐ Morjim beach ⓣ 0832 645 0599 ⓦ www.marbelabeach.com ⓛ 10.00–23.00 daily

Shanti Bar £££ Hugely popular Russian-run bar, lounge and restaurant serving up properly made cocktails from experienced bartenders, along with electronic music by international DJs. ⓐ Asvem–Mandrem beach road ⓣ 98 22 642624 ⓦ www.sashanti.com/shanti ⓛ 10.00–23.00 daily

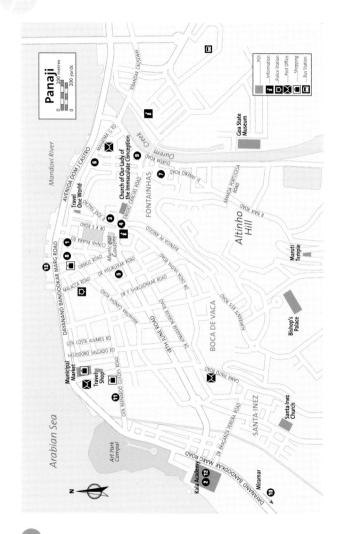

Panaji

0 200 metres
0 200 yards

POI
Information
Police Station
Post Office
Shopping
Bus Station

Mandovi River

Arabian Sea

Art Park Campal

Kala Academy

Municipal Market

Travel Shop

Travel One World

Church of Our Lady of the Immaculate Conception

Municipal Gardens

AVENIDA DOM J. CASTRO

DAYANAND BANDODKAR MARG ROAD

MARITIMA G. PD

CUNHA RIVARA RD

DR E.K. ROAD

ORMUZ ROAD

MALACA ROAD

DR PISURLEKAR ROAD

DR P. SHIRGAONKAR ROAD

MAHATMA GANDHI ROAD

18TH JUNE ROAD

GEN COSTA ALVARES RD

HELIODORO SALGADO RD

GEN BERNARDO GUEDES ROAD

DAYANAND BANDODKAR MARG ROAD

DR. BRAGANZA PEREIRA ROAD

GAMA PINTO ROAD

DR. ATMARAM BORKAR ROAD

AVENIDA DE ANGELO

EMIDIO GRACIAS ROAD

DR OLGA VAIDYA ROAD

J.F. D'SEZ FALCAO

QUEM ROAD

OUREM ROAD

31 JANEIRO ROAD

ARMACA PORTUGUESA ROAD

P. NAIK ROAD

RIBANDAR CAUSEWAY

Ourem Creek

FONTAINHAS

Altinho Hill

Maruti Temple

BOCA DE VACA

ABRANCHES ROAD

Bishop's Palace

SANTA INEZ

Santa Inez Church

Miramar

Goa State Museum

N

52

Panaji

Previously called Panjim, and sometimes still referred to as such, Goa's tiny administrative capital is around 7 km (4½ miles) from the coast, on the banks of the Mandovi River. A bustling town, it has preserved much of its Portuguese heritage, giving it a Mediterranean atmosphere. Thanks to its handiness for the airport, many people who are travelling around the state pass through Panaji at one time or another, and it's different enough from the coastal resorts to keep most of them there for a few days.

Its narrow, often pavement-less cobbled streets are sometimes calm, sometimes noisy with the sounds of trading, traffic and hooting. Colourful little houses with red-tiled roofs and some distinctive public buildings make the capital a pleasant place to stroll around. It also enjoys some of the best cultural, entertainment and dining options, which make a sophisticated change from the identikit shacks at most of the coastal resorts. Much of the action is on the Mandovi River, on whose south bank the city lies. Party boats glide up and down, pumping out bass for all they're worth; for a more serene option you can take a sunset cruise. If your holiday funds are burning a hole in your pocket, you can relieve yourself of them at any one of Goa's many casinos.

BEACHES

Miramar is Panaji's closest beach, just 3 km (2 miles) away, a 40-minute walk along Dayanand Bandodkar Marg. Swimming is safe, but be aware that there can be undercurrents. The beach, sometimes known as Gaspar Dias, affords a good view of Fort Aguada, and you can also spot the occasional dolphin. This is an urban beach so you won't find the same pristine sand and peace as elsewhere.

Dona Paula Beach is 1 km (half a mile) further than Miramar, and often quieter. A popular film location, it offers some watersports and decent shopping. Check with the lifeguards about the undertow before swimming. Caranzalem, in between Dona Paula and Miramar, is better suited to taking the plunge as it has no undercurrents, as is Bambolim,

7 km (4½ miles) from Panaji in the direction of Vasco, a small beach that's popular with Goans. All of these beaches are within a short tuk-tuk ride of Panaji.

THINGS TO SEE & DO

Art Park Campal
Beautifully sculpted city garden with a lake, lanterns in the trees, statues and fountains. Lit up, it's particularly pleasant for an evening stroll. From time to time it is used for art exhibitions.
ⓐ Dayanand Bandodkar Marg

Church of Our Lady of the Immaculate Conception
Bright, white and unmistakable, the church stands proudly overlooking its city, and is particularly impressive when lit up at night. Inside it is simply done out, with a Last Supper scene, two altars and statues of St Peter and St Paul. Mass in English is held at 08.00 from Monday to Friday, and at 08.30 on Sunday. The church is closed to the public during certain services.
ⓐ Emidio Gracias Road ⓒ 09.00–12.30, 15.30–17.30 Mon–Sat, 11.00–12.30, 15.30–17.00 Sun

Goa State Museum
The 12 galleries include sculpture, Christian and religious art, cultural anthropology, furniture, modern art and a photo display on Goa's fight for freedom. You can ask for a guided tour.
ⓐ EDC Complex, by Ourem Creek ⓣ 0832 243 8006/7306 ⓦ www.goamuseum.nic.in ⓔ museum_goa@sancharnet.in ⓒ 09.30–17.30 Mon–Fri, closed Sat & Sun

Maruti Temple
If you can face the 100-plus steps required to get up there, the Maruti Temple, dedicated to the monkey god Hanuman, will reward you, both with its excellent views over Panaji and also with a cool, marble-floored place to sit and recover. If your visit coincides with the priest's

appearance, you can watch some Hindu rituals, while from 16.00 worshippers come to bathe in the water tank. ⓐ Fontainhas ⓣ 0832 242 6090

Trips
Panaji is a good centre from which to book trips to other parts of the state. **Travel Shop** is a government-approved agency offering trips to

⬤ *The illuminated Church of Our Lady of the Immaculate Conception*

various resorts (from around 200 rupees) and tours such as Goa by night, as well as bus services.

🅐 15 Trionara Apartments, 1st floor, near Municipal Market 🕿 0832 223 2020 🅦 www.goatravelshop.com 🅔 hello@goatravelshop.com

Travel One World

🅐 Mhamai Kamat Building, near Old Secretariat 🕿 0832 242 7047/ 92 25 901760 🅔 sonya@traveloneworld.co.in 🕓 09.15–19.30 or 20.00 Mon–Sat, 09.15–16.30 Sun (most but not all)

⬥ *Get great views from the Maruti Temple*

TAKING A BREAK

Cafés

Café Coffee Day £ ❶ Part of a Western-style chain serving coffees, juices, cakes, sandwiches and ice cream, this branch has a balcony. There are also outlets in Calangute and Colva. ⓐ Arthur Viegas Building, next to Hotel Law ⓔ dolly@cafecoffeeday.com ⓛ 09.00–23.00 daily

Kala Academy Café £ ❷ Large covered café at the academy, serving a range of drinks and snacks. ⓐ Dayanand Bandodkar Marg ⓛ 09.00–20.00 daily (later if there is an event)

Mr Baker £ ❸ Cool and airy two-level bakery with a few tables, where you can enjoy a tea, instant coffee, cake and pastry. ⓐ Opposite church, near Municipal Gardens ⓣ 0832 222 4622 ⓛ 08.30–13.00, 15.30–20.00 daily

AFTER DARK

Restaurants

George £ ❹ Cheap, no-frills city restaurant packed with locals, serving predominantly Goan-Catholic food. Seafood dishes such as mackerel recheado and fish curry rice are great, as are the numerous beef and pork options, including the rare treat of pigling roast. ⓐ Near Church of Our Lady of the Immaculate Conception ⓣ 0832 242 6820/98 22 487722 ⓛ 11.00–15.30, 18.30–22.30 Mon–Sat, closed Sun ❶ Credit cards accepted

Ritz Classic £ ❺ Home of the famous fish thali, this Panaji seafood institution has the air of an old 1970s eatery about it. But the food is unbeatable, which is why it's packed out day and night. ⓐ 18th June Road ⓣ 0832 664 4796 ⓛ 12.00–15.00, 19.00–23.00 daily

Vihar £ ❻ Popular vegetarian place serving South Indian and Chinese food. Its juice bar is a big hit, as are its coconut curries. ⓐ 31 Janeiro Road ⓣ 0832 222 5744 ⓛ 07.00–22.00 daily

Viva Panjim £ ❼ Getting seated and served can take time in this intimate courtyard restaurant, prettily lit and decorated with plants. There's an air-conditioned section and small terrace. The fish is particularly recommended. ⓐ 178, 31 Janeiro Road, Fontainhas ❶ 0832 242 2405/98 50 471363 ⓒ 12.00–15.00, 19.00–22.30 daily

Delhi Darbar £££ ❽ Busy North Indian restaurant with an extensive list of vegetarian options. The upstairs floor can get very crowded, but the air conditioning makes that forgivable. ⓐ Dayanand Bandodkar Marg ❶ 0832 222 2544 ⓒ 11.30–15.30, 19.00–23.00 daily ❶ Credit cards accepted

Horseshoe £££ ❾ In a charming bistro setting, chef Vasco Silveira takes the rugged authenticity of Goan-Portuguese village cooking and distils it into a fine art. Grinding all the spices himself, his Chicken Vindahlo and Pork Feijoada are the real deal. Not much suited to vegetarians. ⓐ E-245, Ourem Road ❶ 0832 243 1788 ⓒ 19.00–22.30 Mon, 12.00–14.30 & 19.00–22.30 Tues–Sat, closed Sun

⬤ *Seafood heaven at the Marriott*

Marriott restaurants £££ ❿ The hotel chain's four top-quality restaurants are all in one partially uncovered area, by the swimming pool. Monday, Wednesday and Friday are theme nights. Don't expect to pay Indian prices. ⓐ Miramar Beach, Dayanand Bandodkar Marg ❶ 0832 246 3333 ❶ 0832 246 3300 ⓦ www.marriott.com/goimc ❶ Coffee shop 24 hours daily, Wan Hao Chinese restaurant 19.00–23.00 Tues–Sun, closed Mon, Simply Grilled 19.00–23.00 daily (Nov–Apr), Cake shop 08.00–22.30 daily

Entertainment
Inox Cinema ⓫ Modern luxury cinema that shows both Indian films and the latest Hollywood hits. ⓐ Behind Goa Medical College, Gen Bernardo Guedes Road ❶ 0832 242 0999 ⓦ www.inoxmovies.com ❶ First show 11.00, last show 23.00

Kala Academy ⓬ Modern art academy that hosts concerts, conferences, plays, films, lectures, music and dance courses. There's also an art gallery, library, exhibition centre and a handicraft market. ⓐ Dayanand Bandodkar Marg ❶ 0832 222 3280/0832 242 0452 ⓦ www.kalaacademygoa.org

MV Caravela ⓭ India's first floating casino can be worth a visit even if you have no intention of gambling. The prices are high, but your entrance fee includes drinks, and dinner if you board later. The sunset cruise is from 17.30 to 19.30 daily and costs 500 rupees; dinner is from 19.30. There are age restrictions, so bring ID if you look young. There's also a 'smart-casual' dress code: shorts, three-quarter-length trousers, vests (for men), flip-flops and sandals are not allowed. ⓐ Fisheries Jetty, Dayanand Bandodkar Marg ❶ 0832 223 4044 ⓔ goacas@sancharnet.in ❶ 17.30–05.00 Mon–Thur, 17.30–06.00 Fri–Sun ❶ Admission charge

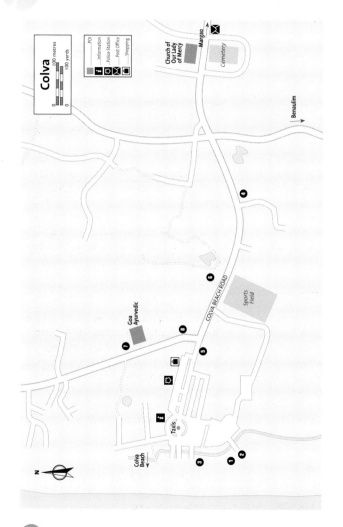

Colva

0 — 100 metres
0 — 100 yards

POI
Information
Police Station
Post Office
Shopping

Church of
Our Lady
of Mercy

Margao

Cemetery

Benaulim

COLVA BEACH ROAD

Goa
Ayurvedic

Sports
Field

Colva
Beach

Taxis

N

Colva

Once a small fishing village, today Colva's merchants are more likely to be trying to hook package tourists. It's the South Goan equivalent of Calangute, although not as developed. There's enough tourist-oriented nightlife for the place to feel like a proper resort, but it's less of a magnet for clubbers than some of the northern resorts, and is consequently popular with a slightly older crowd of holidaymakers, who like their nights out but also want to be in bed before the sun comes up. Plenty of independent market stalls compete with the higher-end shops for your custom, and many of them stay open late into the evening, which means the resort is lively for most of the time, and does not have that post-beach, pre-dinner lull that some smaller places do. It's not the smartest town on the coast, but has an unpolished charm that can appeal to the laid-back traveller. Much of the activity is centred on a big concrete circle; in one direction this leads to the road to Margao and in the other to two small concrete bridges over which lies the beach.

BEACHES

Although now overshadowed by tourism, fishing still plays an important role in Colvan life. There's often some sort of fish-related activity going on at the beach, and early risers can sometimes see the catch being brought in. Most of the activity takes place near the bridges, where the fish vans await their loads and the beach shacks are concentrated. There are also a few funfair-type stalls here. If you're after more seclusion, walk for a few hundred metres; the beach shacks and sunbathers soon thin out. The clean, palm-fringed beach is not particularly wide, but seldom feels too crowded, although more Indian tourists tend to arrive over the weekend and at peak holiday time.

As well as a volleyball net for those who fancy a little beach exercise, some watersports are available in Colva, with the dolphin trip operators particularly dynamic in trying to put tourist bums on their boat seats. However, if you're lucky, you might not even need to take to sea – the

dolphins occasionally venture near enough to the shore to be visible from your sunbed.

The long, uninterrupted stretch of sand around Colva is also good for walkers. Go left along the beach and you'll come to the quieter Benaulim, right and you will ultimately reach the entirely un-touristy Majorda. At night the shoreline becomes lively, with many of the beach shacks trying to outdo each other with their live music.

THINGS TO SEE & DO

Ayurveda
Goa Ayurvedic
ⓐ Longuinos Road, Colva ⓣ 0832 270 0941 ⓦ www.goaayurvedic.com

Church of Our Lady of Mercy
Contains a statue of Baby Jesus, whose finger – attached from a previous statue removed by the Christians – is said to grant miracles. Chief among the hopeful are young singletons seeking a partner.
ⓐ Colva Beach Road, opposite the post office

TAKING A BREAK

Sun Sea & Sand £ ❶   With a good range of juices, milkshakes, lassis, cocktails and 'mocktails', this no-frills beach shack is well placed for you to take on liquids between swimming and sunbathing. ⓐ Colva Beach ⓣ 0832 278 9077 ⓔ antonioseasun@goatelecom.com ⓛ 11.00–19.00 daily

AFTER DARK

Luke's Place £ ❷   With comfy sofas and a bright mural on the back wall, Luke's has a relaxed, slightly alternative vibe. ⓐ Beachfront, sixth shack on right from approach road ⓣ 98 90 225436 ⓔ lukesplace82@yahoo.in ⓛ 10.00–24.00 daily

⬥ *The palm-fringed resort of Colva*

Oceanic Seafood Haven £ ❸   Popular with local families as well
as tourists, Oceanic is a great place to sit and watch the fishermen
go about their work. The service is good, and the food is cheap
and filling. ⓐ On the beach, to left of approach road ❸ 98 81 096570
🕐 08.00–24.00 or last customer, daily

Gatsby's ££ ❹   The only stand-alone pub and disco in South Goa,
Gatsby's also has a 24-hour coffee shop. Peak time is between 21.00
and 03.00. ⓐ Colva Beach Road, next to UTI Bank ❸ 0832 278 9745
🕐 24 hours daily

Goodman's ££ ❺   Run by a Norwegian woman and her Indian husband,
Goodman's draws in holidaymakers with its live music – check the
noticeboard for bands and karaoke – and sports events on the big screen.
It's simply decorated with a few pictures on the wall, and there's a pool
table and dartboard. ⓐ Colva Beach Road ❸ 0832 278 8041
🕐 08.00–24.00 daily

Mickey's ££ ❻   Popular and unpretentious place catering to a fun-
loving, foreign crowd. Unlike a lot of places, Mickey's offers lamb dishes.
ⓐ UBI's Pride Apartments, near sports field ❸ 0832 278 9125
ⓔ mickeyscolvagoa@yahoo.co.in 🕐 12.00–15.00, 18.00–24.00 daily

Sea Pearl ££ ❼   Highly reputed meat-oriented eatery; its pretty fairy
lights and lively atmosphere make it a good choice for dinner. As well
as the seafood, some of the continental staples are not half bad.
ⓐ Opposite Vista-de-Colva ❸ 0832 273 0070 🕐 08.30–14.00, 18.00–
23.00 daily

Tate Sports Bar & Restaurant ££ ❽   New restaurant trying to bring
a touch of sophistication to seaside dining with leather seats and
a sand-free tiled floor. The menu includes English specialities such as
cottage pies, home-made pies, steaks, apple crumble and custard. The
bar is equipped with TVs showing sport, music and a wide selection of

children's games. Popular with the expat community. 🅰 In front of
Skylark Beach Resort 🕿 98 23 615104 🄴 emmaandtoff@hotmail.com
🕓 08.00–24.00 daily

🔺 *Parasols on Colva beach*

Benaulim

Understated Benaulim offers beauty at bargain prices. Despite its proximity to Colva, it is far more serene and relaxed, and many visitors to this resort stay on for weeks or even longer. The nightlife is on the low-key side, and while the place is certainly on the road to greater development, for now you can still enjoy the 'real Goa' here. Larger hotels are only just beginning to appear alongside the paddy fields and ramshackle cottages that give the town its rural feel. That's not to say that everything about Benaulim is low budget and basic. The Taj Exotica ensures that there is plenty of classy dining if you want it. At the other end of the scale, a small Kashmiri market is growing up around the crossroads area in the middle of the village.

BEACHES

Flecked with fishing boats and the odd cow ambling along, Benaulim's beach is a haven of calm. The small approach road hosts a modest market with beach essentials such as flip-flops, sunhats, T-shirts and Frisbees®. You can also pick up your postcards, some Ayurvedic medicine and a coconut juice there. Once you get to the beach, you'll have little trouble finding an empty sunbed. If you want even more seclusion, wander left past the half dozen or so of beach shacks, and you may pretty much have the sand to yourself, apart from the approach of an occasional beach trader. Weekends and holiday times can be busier, since the beach is a favourite with Indian holidaymakers. The sea is safe for swimming, but you should stick to the designated area, where the lifeguard sometimes patrols. A flag system is in operation.

THINGS TO SEE & DO

Manthan

This converted 15-room manor is now run as a heritage gallery, where you can pick up furniture, art, antiques and clothes. Shopping here is not

exactly cheap, but the old building is worth a look round, even if your budget doesn't stretch to actually buying anything.

ⓐ 1346 Manzil Vaddo, near Holy Trinity Church ❶ 0832 277 1659
🕑 09.30–21.00 daily

🔺 *Blissful Benaulim*

Watersports

Colva is the local centre for watersports, but you can still do some activities from Benaulim.

Dolphin trips leave **Pele's Watersports** at 08.00 and 09.00. Fishing, banana-boat trips, jet-skiing and parasailing can also be arranged.

☏ 98 22 080045

⬥ *Dolphins are regular visitors to Benaulim*

TAKING A BREAK

Taj Exotica Poolside Sandwich Counter and Fresh Fruit The place for an upmarket poolside lunch. There's a daily health drink for the diet-conscious and ice cream for the less so. ⓐ Hotel Taj Exotica ⓣ 0832 668 3333 ⓛ 09.00–19.00 daily ⓘ Credit cards accepted

AFTER DARK

Pedro's £ A Benaulim veteran, brightly coloured Pedro's started up in 1969. A British musician plays live on Tuesday while on Saturday it's the turn of a Goan performer to take to the stage. There's a small dance floor, an extensive menu, and the place also organises dolphin trips departing at 08.00 and 09.30. ⓐ By entrance from road ⓣ 982 238 9177 ⓛ 08.00–02.00 daily

Fusion ££ Steak that comes very highly recommended. There is a caveat though: the excellent Brazilian chef has left and returned to the restaurant twice now; when he's there it's great, but when he's not it's hard to know what to expect. It's best to check the situation before turning up. ⓐ Majorda Beach Road ⓣ 98 90 064833 ⓛ 19.00–22.00 daily

Sun and Moon ££ Located near the Taj Exotica, this beach shack has a great reputation for Indian and Chinese cuisine, and a long and dedicated list of customers who return year upon year swear by the friendly service. Has decent cocktails as well as the ubiquitous seafood dishes. ⓐ Near Taj Exotica ⓣ 08.00–23.00 daily

Lobster Shack £££ One of the always impressive Taj Hotel restaurants, this beachfront eatery offers exquisitely prepared fresh fish alongside a live seafood display and open kitchen. Expect the prices to be as international as the standards. ⓐ Hotel Taj Exotica ⓣ 0832 668 3333 ⓛ 11.00–23.00 daily (Sept–May) ⓘ Credit cards accepted

Palolem

In the last few years the scene at Palolem has exploded, with the slow-paced picture-perfect paradise that once existed now largely relegated to the sidelines. True, the gentle curve of the bay can still take the breath away, especially with the rising and setting of the sun, but the sleepy little village that Palolem once was has been replaced with a much more developed tourist town. One welcome consequence of this is the food that's on offer, with no other beach in Goa offering such range and quality in dining options. Another development is the increase in domestic tourism, whether it be the carloads of curious day-trippers from neighbouring states or more involved young urban couples.

Because of the pace of progress, Palolem's life has spilled off into the surrounding beaches, with both Patnem to the south and Agonda to the north becoming destinations in their own right. The former is still very chilled, but Agonda is already becoming rather overcrowded.

BEACHES

The sea here is generally the preserve of fishermen and of swimmers enjoying the gradual slope of the seabed and calm waters. Be aware that there are some undertows, especially at the southern end of the beach; there are signs directing you to a specified bathing area and you will often find a lifeguard on duty. Other water-based activities are pretty much limited to boogie boarding and surfing, or dolphin spotting with one of the local fishermen – and there's a volleyball net on the sand.

But few visitors are here to exert themselves. If you're lying on the beach or taking on refreshments at one of the small beach shacks, you don't even have to get up to buy a book: the book wallah will come to you. Ditto the taxi drivers and boat operators, who congregate at the entrance to the beach.

Although protected from over-exploitation by its distance from the other main resorts, Palolem has increasingly become part of the tourist

trail in recent years. For more solitude, head south: the secluded **Patnem**, **Colomb** and **Rajbag** beaches are all within walking distance.

THINGS TO SEE & DO

Ayurveda
Bhakti Kutir Ayurveda Centre
Choose from massages, detox, consultations with an Ayurvedic doctor, yoga classes, meditation and a circus theatre workshop. There are also lessons for children and language lessons for adults in Hindi and the local tongue, Konkani.
ⓐ 296 Colomb, 200 m (220 yds) from the beach ❶ 0832 264 3469
Ⓦ www.bhaktikutir.com ⓔ bhaktikutir@gmail.com

Bio Veda Ayurvedic Resort
English-run centre that's praised for both its services and prices and its quality accommodation in beach huts.
ⓐ Agonda Beach, 7 km (4½ miles) north of Palolem Beach
❶ 97 64 427191/94 22 388982 Ⓦ www.bioveda.in ⓔ info@bioveda.in

🔺 *Charm and beauty: Palolem*

TAKING A BREAK

Rockit £ The best beach shack in Palolem. The menu is solid, the music smart and the atmosphere exceptional, with boss Clem and the rest of the gang so welcoming and playful that everyone feels like a regular right away. ⓐ Palolem beach, north end ❶ 98 23 928345 ❶ 08.00–23.00 daily

Café Inn ££ Israeli café serving the best coffee in south Goa, along with hearty breakfasts, salads and wraps. In the evenings there's a traditional barbecue with laffa bread and an unlimited supply of ten traditional salads. A great hangout and meeting place. ⓐ Palolem Beach Road junction ⓦ www.cafeinn.in ❶ 10.00–23.00 daily

AFTER DARK

Bars, cafés & restaurants

Alessandra ££ Upmarket Israeli-Indian family-friendly beach huts with Middle Eastern-style lounge area where you can sit, drink and eat away the day. Middle Eastern dishes fill the menu, along with burgers, wraps, salads and desserts. The Brandy Coffee Slush is the stuff of legend. ⓐ Palolem Beach, north end ⓦ www.alessandra-resort.com ❶ 07.00–23.30 daily

Boom Shankar ££ Arguably the best sunset spot in Goa, overlooking the picturesque Columb Bay, this bar and restaurant is known among long-termers for its cheap cocktails. It also serves above-average food, with the spinach and blue cheese crêpe, earthy chicken kolhapuri and fiery Keralan fish pollichathu all winners. ⓐ Columb Bay, south side ❶ 09.00–23.00 daily

Café del Mar ££ Try the daily fresh seafood barbecue, Indian, tandoori and Goan food. All-night bar and live football on the flat-screen TV. ⓐ Palolem Beach ❶ 98 23 276520/313983 ⓦ www.cafedelmar

palolem.com @ info@cafedelmarpalolem © 24 hours daily, last food order 23.00

Cheeky Chapatti ££ A new kind of Anglo-Indian fusion, serving up such tasty intercontinental dishes as beer-battered kingfish and tofu-spinach-mushroom pakora with chilli jam, this wonderfully teak-tented restaurant is one of the most popular in town, so be prepared to wait for your food with a cool beer in hand. Good for breakfast and salads too. @ Palolem main road © 77 98 681393 © 09.00–14.00, 17.00–24.00 daily

Ciaran's ££ Classy beachside hotel restaurant with plush black leather chairs and wooden decking. There's a big book collection and board games to entertain you. Great value and top quality. @ On beach © 0832 264 3477 @ www.ciarans10.com @ hello@ciarans.com © 06.30–23.00 daily, last order 22.30

◐ Dinner on the beach: a perfect end to the day

Dropadi ££ Old-fashioned, no-nonsense Indian restaurant, consistently serving high-quality food while other places rise and fall. The menu is extensive, with a great range of North Indian dishes, but seafood is the prize catch and the fish and prawn dishes won't disappoint.
ⓐ Corner of road and beach ☎ 93 26 127437 ⓦ www.goyam.net
ⓔ sanjaybick@rediffmail.com ⏰ 07.30–23.00 daily, last order at 22.45

Home ££ Enjoy great fresh salads, real Italian coffee and home-made desserts in the welcoming café of this friendly guesthouse. ⓐ Patnem Beach ☎ 0832 264 3916 ⏰ 08.30–21.30 daily

Magic Italy ££ Run by an Italian chef who imports ingredients from home, the pizzas and pastas are made in-house. Magic Italy is bright and colourful, with plants and a pleasant area at the back with cushions. They stick to their area of expertise: Italian food. ⓐ Palolem Beach Road ☎ 0832 2647 0167 ⓦ www.magicitalygoa.com ⏰ 11.30–24.00 daily

Sandy Feet ££ Nepali-run beach shack in neighbouring Agonda, with a wonderfully friendly atmosphere. There are good cocktails, decent backpacker-style Mexican food and a seriously good selection of Nepali cuisine – including a highly recommended, rocket-fuel-spicy chicken salad. ⓐ Agonda Beach, north end ☎ 90 49 114770 ⏰ 09.00–23.00 daily

Hidden Gourmet £££ Five-star cuisine in a romantic, secluded spot on the rocks overlooking Patnem beach. Swiss chef Patrick Buob applies his international training to the wealth of fresh local produce on offer. The emphasis is on seafood but the menu is constantly changing according to the market. ⓐ Colomb rocks, Patnem Beach, north end ☎ 99 23 686185 ⏰ 08.30–15.00, 18.30–22.30 daily

ⓓ *A bird's-eye view of Fort Aguada*

 EXCURSIONS
Out & about

Bardez taluka

Made up of 12 villages plus its capital city, **Mapusa**, Bardez taluka (district) provides a glimpse of a Goa that has nothing to do with tourism, development or cash. A largely rural district, there is no one main attraction: the enjoyment is in driving around – it would be difficult to explore without your own transport – and popping into the tiny temples, churches and villages that you happen upon. In this part of the state, tourists are still a novelty, and you may find yourself something of a curiosity.

GETTING THERE

To get started, take an east turning from National Highway 17, which runs between Panaji and Mapusa. Any local tuk-tuk or taxi driver should know some of the prettier and more interesting spots.

THINGS TO SEE & DO

Houses of Goa Museum

This place showcases Goan architecture through maps, designs and plans, some of which are over 500 years old. There's a slide show at 19.00 and a pleasant café on the ground floor.

ⓐ Torda, Salvador-do-Mundo village ⓣ 0832 241 0711 ⓕ 0832 241 0709
ⓦ www.archgoa.org ⓛ 10.00–19.30 Tues–Sun, closed Mon
ⓘ Admission charge

Mapusa Market

The Mapusa market has something that makes it stand out in the area: it's genuinely Indian. That's not to say there's nothing on offer for the tourist though; on the contrary, the roads and alleyways are full of sights, sounds, smells and bargains, and although there are no hippy wares on offer it's well worth spending a couple of hours wandering around, if only to understand how a real market town works.

ⓐ Mapusa ⓛ 09.00–13.00, 16.00–20.00 daily

TAKING A BREAK

Heera Snacks and Ice Cream £ Ideally situated if you're just getting on or off a bus and want some light refreshments. ⓐ Mapusa, north of the roundabout, opposite the bus station ⓛ 08.00–12.00, 16.00–24.00 daily

Villa Blanche ££ A slice of German village in the middle of Goa, this garden café and bakery has the virtue of sourcing its ingredients via a yearly overland bus journey from Europe to India. ⓐ Assagao village ⓦ http://villablanche-goa.com ⓛ 09.00–17.30 Mon–Sat, 10.00–15.00 Sun

AFTER DARK

Sublime £££ One of the best restaurants in Goa, Sublime combines a wealth of fine local ingredients with the depth of chef Christopher Saleem's international training. There's a good range of steaks on the menu, while the signature dish of clams in marinara with spicy Goan sausage is lick-the-bowl good. ⓐ 1/9-A, Grande Morod, Saligao ⓕ 98 22 484051 ⓛ 11.00–15.00, 18.30–23.00 daily

ⓐ *Jewellery seller at Mapusa market*

Fort Aguada & Sinquerim

Now nearly 400 years old, Aguada was a key fort during the Portuguese occupation, and enjoyed such a superb strategic location that it was never taken by force. Now a protected monument, the fort enjoys splendid views over the coast, and is especially enchanting at sunset. Back down the road at the bottom of the hill is the Aguada jetty, the increasingly crowded and chaotic location of daily boat trips offering early-morning dolphin-watching, fishing jaunts or simple sightseeing excursions. In peak season and on festival days it can be gridlock, so if you want a peaceful trip that's free of excitable tourists it's best to arrive way before 09.00.

GETTING THERE

Energetic and hardy types can reach the fort on foot by a trail that starts at Marbella Guesthouse, but it's a very steep 2-km (1¼-mile) climb. Otherwise the 4-km (2½-mile) journey from Sinquerim can be done by bicycle, motorcycle or taxi.

THINGS TO SEE & DO

Most visitors make for the old bastion, on the top of the hill. Here you can see the enormous subterranean water tanks that would have sustained the fort in the event of a long siege. The old four-storey Portuguese lighthouse is another point of interest, said to be the oldest of its kind in India. The new lighthouse is open to visitors from 16.00 to 17.30 for a small charge.

Boat trips

There are plenty of organised tours back in town but you can also just turn up at the jetty and bargain hard for the kind of trip you want. In the early morning there's a very good chance of seeing dolphins off the headland. You can also arrange your own private fishing trips. The price is roughly 1,000 rupees upward for private hire, regardless of the number of people.

● The former Portuguese stronghold of Fort Aguada

TAKING A BREAK

Veronica's Fish Cutlets £ Among the nondescript food and drink stalls around the Aguada-Sinquerim jetty, Veronica Fernandes sells her locally famous fish cutlets (among other snacks), served up in a burger bun with spicy coconut chutney for mind-bogglingly low prices. They sell out within a couple of hours, so snap one up after an early-morning boat trip. **ⓐ** Sinquerim/Aguada jetty **ⓛ** 09.00–13.00 daily

The Curry House ££ With a pleasant, mellow atmosphere and occasional live music, the Curry House dishes up the typical range of food with an emphasis – obviously – on curry. **ⓐ** Fort Aguada Road, near Kingfisher Villa, Dando **ⓣ** 98 90 481096 **ⓛ** 09.00–01.00 daily

The Stone House ££ The food here gets good write-ups, and the weekly live music, sometimes jazz and blues, creates a cool atmosphere. **ⓐ** Fort Aguada Road **ⓣ** 0832 247 9909 **ⓛ** 07.00–24.00 daily (Oct–Mar)

Sweet Chilli ££ This garden restaurant has a lively atmosphere boosted by regular theme nights. Outside the holiday season it's only open over the weekend. The food comes highly recommended. **ⓐ** Off the Taj Fort Aguada junction **ⓣ** 0832 247 9446 **ⓔ** sweetchillilounge@rediffmail.com **ⓛ** 09.00–23.00 daily

Morisco £££ A daily-changing menu and an open kitchen are two of the draws at this superior seafood restaurant. There's live entertainment in the evenings from October to March. Sip a fresh watermelon Martini while enjoying panoramic views over the ocean and fort at their new bar, SFX. **ⓐ** Vivantabytaj, Fort Aguada Beach Resort **ⓣ** 0832 664 5858 **ⓛ** 19.30–23.00, SFX 11.00–23.00 daily **ⓘ** Credit cards accepted

Dr Salim Ali Bird Sanctuary

Providing sanctuary not only for Goa's feathered friends, this wildlife reserve also offers human visitors a respite from the noise and bustle of the resorts. Taking its name from the so-called 'Birdman of India', the country's most famous ornithologist, the bird sanctuary makes a good half-day trip. Bird lovers have more obvious reasons to go there, but floating slowly around the creeks in a boat, with no other human in sight apart from your boatman, offers an enchanting glimpse of rural India.

GETTING THERE

Getting there requires some effort. Take the ferry from Ribandar, 4 km (2½ miles) from Panaji, across the Mandovi River to Chorao island. Ferries run every ten minutes in each direction from 06.00–02.00. From the disembarking point you can walk to the sanctuary. Buy your ticket at the small office to the left.

ⓐ By ferry wharf ⓒ Office open 09.00–17.00 daily ❶ Admission charge

THINGS TO SEE & DO

To make the most out of your trip, it's best to hire a boatman, who will probably be hanging around at the wharf waiting for tourists. After negotiating a price, he'll take you to the vessel, a hollowed-out mango tree that can hold up to four passengers. The sanctuary itself is less than 200 ha (494 acres) in total but, despite its small size, is home to some 400 different bird species, among which you're likely to spot egrets, cormorants, herons, kingfishers, kites, eagles and woodpeckers. The odd otter, jackal or crocodile may also be visible. A good viewing point is the birdwatching tower, but access to this is dependent on the water level.

Perhaps because it's somewhat out of the way, few tourists reach the sanctuary, and you may well find you are sharing the mangrove-lined

waterways only with the wildlife you're there to see and the odd fishing boat attending to its nets.

The sanctuary is open all year round, but is at its best – in terms both of birds and of heat and humidity – from October to March or April. The ideal time of day to visit is early in the morning, from 06.00 to 09.00, and from 17.00 until dusk. Not having a constant stream of tourists, there are no real facilities to speak of, but you can find a few places to stop for a tea or a juice, usually open from around 06.30 to 20.30.

TAKING A BREAK

Tukram Mandrekar fresh lime soda shop £ Small, no-frills place where you can pick up a fresh lime soda. ➌ Near ferry 🕘 08.00–20.30 daily

🔺 *Crocodiles are among the wildlife visible at the sanctuary*

Old Goa

Old Goa is the antidote to the undemanding beach life – here you will find culture and history in spades. In its heyday, the city, chosen by the Portuguese as their capital, was the size of London, and rivalled Lisbon in its greatness. But while what stands today is not on that scale, Old Goa's buildings are impressive enough to capture the grandeur of its history; its churches and convents are listed as a UNESCO World Heritage Site. The attractions, mostly opulent churches, are centred on a large, neat green. Be warned – there is very little shade when walking between them.

GETTING THERE

The town is 9 km (5½ miles) east of Panaji, from where you can pick up a bus at the Kadamba bus stand. Buses depart frequently and take just under half an hour. You can also continue by bus to Ponda.

THINGS TO SEE & DO

Archaeology Museum

Sculptures, paintings and fragments, mostly with a religious theme, are on display. Some exhibits date back over 2,000 years.
ⓐ Adjoining the Church of St Francis of Assisi ❶ 0832 228 5302
🕐 10.00–17.00 Sat–Thur, closed Fri ❶ Admission charge; children under 15 go in for free

Basilica of Bom Jesus

Probably the most impressive of Old Goa's churches, the basilica is the resting place of the remains of the missionary St Francis Xavier, co-founder of the Jesuits, whose feast day (3 Dec) is a big celebration in and around Old Goa. The 17th-century Baroque building has marble floors, inlaid in places with precious stones and richly gilded altars.
ⓐ 100 m (110 yds) south of Old Goa Road 🕐 08.30–17.30 daily

⬥ *The Church of St Francis of Assisi*

Bom Jesus Basilica Art Gallery

The Bom Jesus Basilica Art Gallery is the largest gallery of modern church
art in Asia, featuring paintings commissioned and executed in the 1970s.
🅰 Upstairs at Basilica of Bom Jesus 🕘 09.00–17.00 Wed–Mon,
closed Tues

Church of St Francis of Assisi

This high-ceilinged church has a stunning interior, thanks to both its
gold and the big paintings on the walls.
🅰 250 m (275 yds) north of Old Goa Road, in between Chapel of
St Catherine and Sé Cathedral 🕘 09.00–17.30 daily

Kristu Kala Mandir Art Gallery

Much of the religious art here is of a modern bent, including the life-size wax model of the Last Supper. There's a pleasant garden at the back.

🅐 Adjoining the Sé Cathedral 🕐 09.30–17.30 Tues–Sun, closed Mon

❗ Admission charge

🔺 *The striking Sé Cathedral*

Sé Cathedral

One of the largest churches in Asia, the Sé Cathedral has a striking white-and-gold interior and stone floor. It also houses the cross of miracles, on which shepherds are said to have seen an apparition of Christ in 1619. ❸ In same complex as Church of St Francis of Assisi 🕒 06.30–17.30 daily

TAKING A BREAK

Asi Canteen £ With a couple of tables, this is one of the only oases in the middle of Old Goa where you can recover with a snack and a drink and take refuge from the unrelenting sun. ⓐ By Sé Cathedral 🕒 06.00–19.00 daily

Solar Souto Maior £ It would be a shame to come without seeing this place, a true highlight of Old Goa. Formerly part of a Portuguese palace, it has retained its stateliness, and is now a delightful complex. The three tables on the charming terrace are nicely spaced out to allow you some privacy. The reasonably priced food is excellent, with the almond soup quite exquisite. You can buy or drink a range of luxury teas in the tearoom, or pick up expensive pashminas, clothes, furniture or gifts from the shop. ⓐ Peres House, HNo B40, St Pedro, 1.5 km (1 mile) from Old Goa 🕒 Café from 10.00–18.00 daily

Ponda

For the tourist, Ponda is about two things: temples and spices. There are five important temples in Ponda, rebuilt after destruction by the Portuguese. Tours of its spice farms are well organised, informative and entertaining. Ponda itself is industrial and busy with traffic and traders, something of a culture shock after the laid-back resorts, although unexpectedly beautiful monuments and statues punctuate the factories and industrial parks.

THINGS TO SEE & DO

Spice farms
Sahakari Spice Farm Very well-organised facility that offers fascinating interactive tours of the spice farm followed by a buffet lunch. It's very touristy, but the professional and knowledgeable guides give you a great time. On Wednesday, Saturday and Sunday you can also have an Ayurveda body massage, and elephant rides and feeding are sometimes possible behind the farm.
🅐 Ponda belgaum Highway Curti 🕿 0832 231 2394/98 50 466478
🅦 www.sahakarifarms.com 🅔 info@sahakarifarms.com 🕒 09.00–last entrance around 16.30 daily

Savoi Plantation
🅐 Savoi, Ponda 🕿 0832 234 0272 🅦 www.savoiplantation.com

Tropical Spice Plantation
🅐 Arla Bazar, Keri 🕿 0832 234 0329 🅔 tropicalspiceplantation@rediffmail.com 🕒 08.00–17.00 daily

Temples
Ponda managed to elude Portuguese control for two and a half centuries after the arrival of the Europeans, and Hindus fleeing persecution elsewhere in the state built the temples to house the deities they had

Ride or feed an elephant at Sahakari Spice Farm...

⬓ *...then break for a buffet*

managed to bring with them. The best one is probably **Sri Manguesh Temple**, off the National Highway 4A, a big complex with chandeliers and a lamp tower. Less than 2 km (1¼ miles) away is **Shri Mahalsa**, a Vishnu temple boasting what is said to be the biggest oil lamp in the world outside it. **Shantadurga Temple**, less than 5 km (3 miles) from the town centre, is one of the biggest and most highly renowned in the state. Its chandelier and polished marble floors and pillars are the most striking features.

TAKING A BREAK

Niranjan Sweet Mart £ It's more of a shop than a sit-in place, but the helpful employees will be delighted to furnish you with a selection of their traditional Indian sweets and cakes. ⓐ Bhavani Sadan, Upper Bazaar ⓣ 0832 231 4412 ⓛ 08.00–20.00 daily

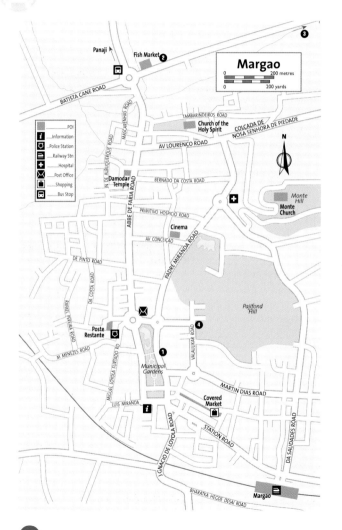

Panaji ↖   Fish Market ②

Margao
0 ____ 200 metres
0 ____ 200 yards

BATISTA CANE ROAD

TAMBARINDEIROS ROAD

Church of the Holy Spirit

COLCADA DE NOSA SENHORA DE PIEDADE

AV LOURENCO ROAD

N

MASCARENHAS ROAD

IN DE ALBUQUEQUE ROAD

Damodar Temple

BERNADO DA COSTA ROAD

Monte Hill

ABBE DE FARIA ROAD

PRIMITIVO HOSPICIO ROAD

Monte Church

Cinema

AV CONCEICAO

DE PINTO ROAD

PADRE MIRANDA ROAD

DA COSTA ROAD

Pajifond Hill

RAFAEL PEREIRA ROAD

Poste Restante

VALAULIKAR ROAD

④

M. MENEZES ROAD

①

MIGUEL LOYOLA FURTADO RD

Municipal Gardens

MARTIN DIAS ROAD

LUIS MIRANDA

Covered Market

DA SAUDADES ROAD

IGNACIO DE LOYOLA ROAD

STATION ROAD

Margao

BHARATKA HEGDE DESAI ROAD

Legend:
- POI
- ℹ️ ....Information
- 🚓 ....Police Station
- 🚆 ....Railway Stn
- ➕ ....Hospital
- ✉️ ....Post Office
- 🛍️ ....Shopping
- 🚌 ....Bus Stop

③

90

Margao

Hectic Margao makes few concessions to tourism, and as such is a good way to experience authentic Indian daily life. There are a couple of markets – with not a hippy bag in sight – some religious sites, plus plenty of Portuguese architecture. All this combines to form a microcosm of Goa as it is outside the beach resorts. If you're heading south by car or bus you're almost certain to pass through Margao, and it's well worth making a short stop.

THINGS TO SEE & DO

Covered market
The sights, smells and sounds of India will besiege you in Margao's vibrant covered market. Spices and fruit are piled up alongside flower garlands and sweets plus a miscellany of practical items like saris, clothes and kitchenware. Goan matriarchs thread through the narrow walkways between stalls, which are crammed in so tightly that the vendors are often sitting atop them with their goods. As much performance artist as

● *Portuguese architecture is among Margao's attractions*

vendor, watch out for the coconut-juice man, whose skills with a machete border on the scary – beware of bits of flying coconut.

ⓐ F de Loiola Road, east of Municipal Gardens ⓗ 08.00–20.00 Mon–Sat, closed Sun

Damodar Temple

Colourful temple with paper flags hanging from the ceiling and portraits on the wall that distinguish it from the norm. The priest is there 07.00–09.00 and 20.30–22.00.

ⓐ Abbe de Faria Road ⓗ 07.30–22.00 daily

🔺 Fish and coconut: staples of the Goan diet

Fish market

It's unlikely you'll want to buy anything from the fish market, but if you're in the area, which is likely due to its proximity to the bus station, do take a look: it provides a real glimpse of authentic Goan life.
ⓐ North of roundabout, opposite bus stop ⏱ Irregular

Heritage homes

Travel inland past Margao into the talukas of Quepem and Salcete and you'd be forgiven for thinking you've entered another Goa entirely. Here tourism drops off to virtually nothing, the beach resorts become a memory, and the towns and villages that unfold are full of a still-living Portuguese and Hindu past. Along with the many abandoned and well-maintained private villas there are a number of heritage homes that are open to the public, each one with a distinct appeal and story of its own.

The most famous of these is perhaps the west wing of the **Braganza Mansion** (the Casa Menezes-Braganza section) in Chandor (ⓐ 9 km/6 miles east of Margao ☎ 0832 278 4201 ⏱ 10.00–17.00 Mon–Sat, closed Sun), an impeccably maintained piece of Portuguese-Goan grandeur presided over by the ageing matriarch Dona Aida.

Just down the road there's also the **Fernandes House** (ⓐ 136 Cotta Chandor, 500 m/550 yds east of Braganza Mansion ☎ 98 22 952698 ⏱ 09.00–18.00 daily), a ramshackle but no less interesting building, with ancient Hindu artefacts, secret passageways and swords on display.

Further south, in Quepem, is the **Palacio do Deao** (ⓐ opposite Holy Cross Church ☎ 0832 266 4029 ⏱ 10.00–18.00 daily), with its ornate gardens and beautiful interiors that have been lovingly and painstakingly restored by owners Ruben and Celia Vasco da Gama.

Municipal Gardens

Margao's pretty gardens are a small haven from the bustle of city life, and sleepy Margaons can often be seen having a lie-down in the shade. There's a water feature, a variety of flowers and benches, as well as a children's play area.

② Between Abbe de Faria Road and Padre Miranda Road, south of the post office **🕐** 07.30–20.30 daily

TAKING A BREAK

Café Marliz £ ❶ This quirkily decorated café doesn't serve main meals, but it's a decent place to have a juice. **②** Next to Municipal Gardens **🕐** 15.00–19.30 daily

AFTER DARK

Damodar's ££ ❷ Clean, simple and air-conditioned, this family restaurant serves Goan, Indian and Chinese meals with a lot of fish. Cool down afterwards with an ice cream or juice. **②** First floor of complex next to fish market **📞** 0832 270 0511 **🕐** 11.00–16.00, 19.00–23.00 daily

Fernando's Nostalgia ££ ❸ Close to Margao in the village of Raia, Fernando's Nostalgia is a delightful link to the past, where owner Margarida flits from table to table, keeping her late husband's dream of Goan-Portuguese food alive. Salted ox-tongue, stuffed and baked crabs and squid rechiado are delicious as well as being hard to find anywhere else. **②** 608 Uzro Raia, Salcete **📞** 0832 277 7054 **🕐** 11.00–15.00, 19.00–23.00 daily

Gaylin ££ ❹ This newly renovated Chinese restaurant is done out with the required lanterns, dragons and so on. It's a relaxed place to eat with a pleasant staff, and the air-conditioned ground floor is a big draw. **②** Shar-N-Shorai Building, Valaulikar Road **📞** 0832 273 3348 **🕐** 11.00–15.00, 19.00–24.00 daily

▶ *Colourful crafts reflect Goan culture*

LIFESTYLE
The Goan way

Food & drink

Like its architecture, festivals, religions and much else besides, Goa's food is a melange of different influences. On the one hand, it's part of India, and the nation's love of eye-watering spices, rice, lentils and chutneys informs Goan gastronomy. On the other hand, the state often has the feel of an island, and its distinct identity is also reflected in local dishes, as is the huge natural resource to which Goan restaurateurs have unlimited access: the sea. Even inland Goa is dissected by rivers, and fish is a staple of the state's cuisine.

The classic dish is probably fish curry, which you'll see on practically every menu in every resort. Other seafood curries are also popular, and the Portuguese have also influenced the way Goans eat it: *caldeirada* (fish stew with various vegetables and herbs, cooked in wine) and *recheiado* (fried fish with a spicy masala filling) are two gastronomic colonial legacies. Sea creatures that could end up on your plate include kingfish, tuna, shark, rockfish, sardines, pomfret, mackerel, squid and mussels. Many restaurants can also do you tiger prawns or lobster, provided that you order in advance; some dedicate one night of the week to each.

Committed carnivores should not be put off by India's love of vegetarianism: there's plenty of meat available. While beef is forbidden to Hindus and pork to Muslims, the relaxed Goans seem to place more emphasis on hospitality than asceticism, and most restaurants in tourist resorts, especially the larger establishments, offer both. Chicken also appears extensively on menus, as do goat (sometimes listed as mutton) and – to a lesser extent – lamb. Cooking methods are a mixture of traditional Indian and Portuguese. Many of the dishes are heavily spiced (pepper, garlic, chillies, turmeric, coriander, cumin and ginger pop up fairly frequently), although Goan waiters are aware that foreign palates are not as robust as their own, and meals may be prepared far less piquantly than the authentic version. Of course, if your tongue is up to the challenge, they will happily cook you up a local spice-fest too. Spice devotees who are keen to learn more about Goan seasoning should head to one of the spice farms in Ponda.

As in the rest of India, the rule is pretty much 'rice with everything'. Rice is a staple, and is also the best treatment if you've just inadvertently bitten into a particularly tear-inducing chilli. As well as being served separately, rice is also an integral part of many dishes such as the Muslim biryani. Vegetables too play a big part, often in the form of lentils and pulses (*dhal*) or chutneys and relishes, which can also be on the hot side.

While Goa's spicier offerings can be friend or foe to the traveller, there will be few visitors to the state who won't delight in the variety and quality of fruit on offer. The fresh pineapples, watermelons, mangos, papayas and coconuts available are far superior to the versions that make it on to Western supermarket shelves. Buy fruit from one of the

◆ *Fruit and vegetable market in Candolim*

women who wander the beaches with baskets of it on their head, or sample it in the many juices, milkshakes, smoothies or lassis on offer in almost every eatery. The fruit alone may be enough to keep your sweet tooth satisfied, but, if not, the local desserts include *bebinca* (traditional layered pudding that is required eating at all Goan celebrations), *dodol* (a sweet and sticky flour snack with coconuts and cashews) and *kulkuls* (a deep-fried dough featuring – as usual – coconut). If you pass a sweet shop – which is fairly likely, as there are plenty of them around – it's well worth asking for a selection box. There are familiar options such as shortbread and marzipan, and there are plenty of other delicacies that will go down well with everyone, especially with children.

When it comes to drinks, tea is king. Goans – indeed almost all Indians – love their *chai*, and you'll often see the *chai* wallah weaving his way through the street or market with a tray of tea for the traders. Tea in India is milky and indescribably sugary. If that's not to your taste, make sure you ask for the milk and sugar separately – most of the better restaurants will bring it that way automatically. The domination of tea means that coffee takes something of a back seat. It's usually available, although it is not likely to be anything more inspiring than a cup of instant from one of the standard brands; however, some of the better cafés are waking up to the fact that many tourists enjoy their coffee, and now serve a decent cup of filter coffee, espresso or cappuccino.

If you're after something cold, the traditional Indian choice is the lassi, a yoghurt drink that can come in sweet or savoury forms and in Goa is often flavoured with fruit. Because of the heat you'll probably find yourself taking a lot of water on board as well. Juices are ubiquitous, and a range of smoothies and shakes can also be found on most menus. It's worth trying coconut water as much for the show as for the drink itself: the vendor will thwack lumps off the fruit with a huge and rather frightening machete before piercing it with a straw. When you've finished the juice, he will then cut it open for you to eat the flesh.

With a taste more akin to paint stripper than anything else, *feni*, the local spirit, is best taken with some Limca or Sprite. If you prefer your drinks less potent, beer is widely available, with Kingfisher the most

popular brand among tourists. Not subject to the same taxes as it is in the rest of India, it's relatively cheap. Perhaps because of the temperatures, there's less demand for wine, but you can find it in some of the more upmarket restaurants. Much of the liquor consumed in Goa is in the form of cocktails, and most beach shacks will have an extensive list, both alcoholic and non-alcoholic (mocktails).

You can start eating early in Goa; most places open for breakfast at 07.00 or 08.00, some even earlier. The vast majority of restaurants and cafés serve main meals and snacks until 23.00, or later. There's little to choose between the majority of places, which all do English breakfasts, sandwiches and salads, plus standard Indian, Goan, Chinese and continental mains, the latter usually consisting of some pizza and pasta dishes and variations on meat and two veg. Prices are fairly uniform wherever you go, and few places attempt to offer something above and beyond the norm – which means those that do are truly special (and expensive).

Pretty much everything is done with the tourist in mind. While Indians eschew cutlery to eat with their right hand, this is not expected of foreign customers, and you would have to go to the smallest, most off-the-beaten-track local establishment to find a menu that wasn't in English. Since the 2008 smoking ban, non-smokers will be delighted to see that many restaurants display no-smoking signs. However, this rule is seldom respected in practice – the same places often have ashtrays on the tables.

Menu decoder

INDIAN STAPLES

Chaat Savoury snacks served with sweet and spicy chutneys

Chaval, **chawu**, **bhat** Rice

Dahi Yoghurt

Dudh Milk

Masko Butter

Naan Indian flat bread

Paan Betel leaf stuffed with supari (betel nut), quick-lime paste, kathechu paste, gulukand (rose-petal preserve), fennel seeds and dried grated coconut, eaten after a meal to aid digestion

Paneer Indian cottage cheese

Roti Bread

Shakar Sugar

Tatee, **aanda** Egg

Vindalho Chilli and palm vinegar red curry

MAIN COURSES

Aadd maas Pork bones cooked in red spicy gravy

Ambot tik Sour and spicy fish or meat curry with tamarind

Assad roast Goan pork roast

Balchão Very spicy fish or pork dish in tomato sauce

Biryani Spiced saffron rice with pieces of lamb, chicken or vegetables

Caldinha Meat or vegetables cooked in coconut milk, garlic, ginger and chillies

Chicken Cafreal Chicken prepared with a chilli, coriander and garlic marinade and fried

Chouriço Spicy Portuguese smoked sausage

Feijoada Pungent gravy dish of sausage and dried beans

Isvon recheado Kingfish stuffed with chillies and spices in vinegar

Korma Mild curry, with chicken or vegetables, in coconut or yoghurt sauce

Sorpotel Spicy pork dish including the pig's organs

COOKING METHODS

Balti Indian wok or pot

Bhuna, **bhunao**, **jal frezi** Sautéed or stir-fried

MEAT & FISH

Chaamp Chop

Gosht Lamb or beef

Jinga Prawns or shrimp
Khurzi Lamb or chicken with spicy stuffing
Macchi, macchli Fish
Murgh Chicken
Yakhni Mutton

FRUIT & VEGETABLES
Aloo Potato
Aam Mango
Brinjal Aubergine
Gajar Carrot
Kakadi Cucumber
Kela Banana
Matter, mutter Green peas
Naryal Coconut
Neem Ayurvedic medicinal herb
Nimboo Lime
Palak, saag, sag Spinach or green leafy vegetable
Papita Papaya
Phala, phal Fruit
Piaz, peeaz, pyaz Onion
Sabzi Generic term for vegetables
Tarbuz, tarbuj Watermelon

PULSES, NUTS & SEEDS
Channa Chickpea
Badam Almond
Dhal Lentils or lentil soup
Kaju, kajoo Cashew nut

Meve Nuts
Rai Mustard seed
Urad A type of lentil

SPICES & SEASONING
Adrak Ginger
Dalchini, darchim Cinnamon
Dhania Coriander
Lasan Garlic
Mirch Pepper
Namak Salt

DESSERTS
Bebinca Traditional layered pudding with nutmeg, coconut and jaggery
Dodol Thick, sweet and sticky Malaysian dessert with coconut milk, rice flour, jaggery and cashews
Kulkuls Fried dough snack often coated in syrup and traditionally made at Christmas

DRINKS
Chai Indian tea
Feni Powerful Goan spirit made from cashews or coconut
Lassi Cool yoghurt and water drink
Sharab Alcohol/liquor
Udok, pani Water

Shopping

The standard advice for visitors to Goa is to go there with an empty suitcase, which you can then fill throughout your trip with various bargain buys. Shopping is a highlight, not only because what's on offer is such good value, but also because the state's markets – from the huge hippy bazaar at Anjuna to the hotchpotch collections of stalls that cluster around most tourist areas – are a cultural experience in themselves.

Shopping in Goa isn't entirely market-based. As the state continually adapts to the influxes of foreign visitors and the subsequent rise of domestic tourism, some big-name Western clothes stores have sprung up, particularly in the towns frequented by the most tourists, such as the capital Panaji (try the Mahatma Gandhi Road and 18th June Road) and Calangute. Many of the higher-profile brands manufacture their goods in the region, and so prices can be a fair bit lower than you'd expect to pay at home.

Visiting the state's markets – whether you're buying or not – gives all your five senses a blast of Goa. The best ones are alive with colourful products, and noisy with bargaining, begging and bagpipes. Vendors weave around the stalls peddling cakes, drinks and ice creams, all to a perpetual backdrop of competing music and incense sticks. Markets showcase Goa at its most vivid.

The state's most famous market – and a tourist attraction in its own right – is the Wednesday market at Anjuna. Shopping here is an intense experience, and on your arrival the immediate approach of beggars and hawkers can be rather overwhelming. But steel yourself and practise a firm 'no' and you'll soon get into the spirit of things: there are also plenty of places to stop for a breather and some refreshments when you're worn out. Saturday night bazaars in Arpora and Baga are less full on, and you'll have the advantage of being able to shop in the relative cool of the evening. As well as the main tourist ones, it's also worth checking out some of the markets used by Goans. You might not pick up any souvenirs there, but they give you a flavour of a more authentic way of life in the

state, if you fancy getting off the tourist trail. And aside from the official markets, most places have a few stalls selling a motley collection of T-shirts, bags, sunglasses and similar.

With average wages across India low (many of the goods you will see on sale will come from outside Goa), almost everything on sale will seem a bargain. The exception is imported goods, but they are not usually top of foreign visitors' shopping lists. However, your obvious foreignness will work against you, and while few traders are out to con you as such, they naturally want to get as much as they can for what they sell. Whether you're at Anjuna market in full swing or at a lone street stall, it's almost always worth bargaining. The vendor knows that the cost of things in your home country is probably far higher than in Goa, and will fix his or her opening price accordingly. Follow the usual haggling rules. Ask around to find out what prices things usually go for, don't express too

⬢ *Bag yourself a bargain at a local market*

much eagerness over the particular item you want and make as if to walk away if the vendor won't come down far enough. However, do remember to keep things in perspective, and bear in mind that the amount you're negotiating over is probably just a pound or two, which will make very little difference to your holiday funds, but a lot of difference to an Indian trader.

If you're not a fan of bartering, some shops, particularly in the larger towns, do charge fixed, marked prices. This is less common at markets, although a few of the Western vendors, aware of some of their compatriots' discomfort with the bargaining culture, also use such a system. The posher stores selling foreign clothes will also have set prices.

Various souvenirs are on offer. Most prominent are clothes, such as holiday T-shirts and hats with Goa emblazoned across them, plus the hippy-chic range of flowing skirts, floaty tops and floppy hats. There's also an assortment of accessories, such as shoes, jewellery and bags, much of which – again – has a hippy theme. As you'd expect in India, textiles also feature quite prevalently, from small cushion covers to big bedspreads and everything in between, including material for clothesmaking if you prefer to do it yourself. Another option is to use the services of a tailor, which is fairly common practice in Goa, as across India. You won't be restricted to saris – many places will make Western business suits. Other staples include spices, incense sticks, CDs and general Indian bric-a-brac, as well as the standards that you might find in markets everywhere, such as sunglasses, cigarettes, lighters and wallets. Stalls in the coastal resorts usually also have a few inflatables, towels and flip-flops.

One word of warning: some taxi drivers will reduce your fare if you agree to visit a certain shop (which will reward the driver with a kickback). These places can often be very pleasant, air-conditioned and with professional, attentive service (serving plenty of cups of tea). The downside is that prices can be extortionate and you really get the hard sell, so leaving without buying anything can be somewhat awkward. If you don't like this kind of situation, it's worth refusing the driver's discount and avoiding the shop.

Children

Goa is massively popular with families. Golden beaches, reliable weather and relatively low prices tempt parents to all the coastal resorts, while some of the northern beach towns are big draws for mums and dads of a hippy persuasion who want to introduce their outlandishly named offspring to their subculture. Family is central to Indian society, and most groups of local tourists will include at least one small child, so you will seldom feel out of place when travelling as a family. Goa is, if anything, even more child friendly than elsewhere in the country, and the laid-back casualness of most of the restaurants and beach shacks is ideal when you have young kids in tow. Beach shacks are also well suited to watchful parents, allowing them to take a break with a drink while keeping an eye

🔺 *Coast plus children equals fun*

on the children as they play on the beach. However, if you are breastfeeding you should be sensitive to local attitudes: Indian women virtually never expose flesh – they even swim in the sea fully clothed – so exposing a breast, even to feed a child, is likely to be frowned upon. If you need to breastfeed in public, it's best to find a secluded spot.

The obvious entertainment for children is the beach. During the holiday season the sea is often calm enough even for weak swimmers, though of course you will want to look out for the flag system and note the presence or absence of a lifeguard. When they tire of scrabbling around in the sand and paddling, there are plenty of other beach-based activities. Boats go out from most of the busier resorts – the dolphin-spotting trips are a particular winner with children – and teenagers may well want to try some of the higher-octane pursuits like parasailing and jet-skiing, while younger family members can all get a lot of fun out of snorkelling. Hotels – particularly the more expensive ones – often have programmes of entertainment for children, and you may also find ad-hoc classes and activities at the resorts. Keep an eye out for posters advertising what's on, or ask other families.

Wildlife is another big attraction for young holidaymakers. There are several animal and bird sanctuaries in the state, the majority of which are inland. Elephant rides, which are on offer at some of the animal sanctuaries and at a handful of other tourist spots, usually go down well with children, and they can also bathe elephants if sitting on top of one seems a bit too scary. Crocodile trips are also available for the more adventurous.

Sports & activities

Some visitors to Goa may want to do no more than lie on the beach, but if you do tire of sunbathing there are plenty of other options.

CULTURE
Renowned as it is for its pristine beaches and hedonistic party scene, it's sometimes easy to forget that Goa is part of a much larger country with a vast culture. Get away from the hotel strip and the beach and you will find curious little temples, gleaming white churches, centuries-old forts and museums, plus a rich heritage of art, architecture and music. It would be a shame to leave the state without having acquired a sense of its culture and history – along with the tan.

NATURE
There are several national parks, wildlife sanctuaries and protected areas in Goa, as well as some excellent birdwatching sites, particularly close to water and forests. You can find out more at
🌐 www.goaforest.com

WATERSPORTS
The beach itself is the starting point for a lot of what's on offer. In the larger resorts – and sometimes even in the smaller ones too – there is a vast array of watersports catering for everyone from the laid-back to adrenalin junkies. Jet-skiing, waterskiing, windsurfing, parasailing, scuba diving, snorkelling, kite-surfing and kayaking are all tirelessly promoted by young men who roam the beaches, and you can also find more established operators with offices on or near the beach. The main watersport centres are Sinquerim, Calangute, Baga, Colva, and to some extent Benaulim, but even the smaller resorts usually offer a handful of activities. There are also boat trips available for fishing, dolphin spotting and sunset sails. In Panaji an entirely different kind of boat trip attracts tourists, who gamble on the city's floating casinos, or party on one of the booming disco boats. Away from the water, cricket and football are both

◆ *Transport yourself to yoga heaven*

hugely popular throughout Goa and, whether you intend to watch or play, you should find opportunities.

YOGA & AYURVEDA

If all this sounds rather exhausting, at the other end of the scale is the relaxing world of yoga, meditation and Ayurveda, the traditional Indian healing system. Treatments and classes are ubiquitous – you can even have an Ayurvedic massage on the beach in some places, although, as with anything, you get what you pay for. Yoga classes are particularly prevalent in the northern resorts that are more popular with hippies and backpackers, and tend to be advertised on noticeboards around town and in cafés and restaurants. How much time you want to devote to it is up to you. If you're on a short trip or are just curious, pass an hour at a yoga class or 30 minutes treating yourself to a massage. Devotees meanwhile can spend weeks following a thorough programme that includes advice on eating the right foods alongside the exercise.

Festivals & events

Both Hinduism and Christianity have played a vital part in shaping modern Goa, and the legacy is a plethora of different festivals. Unlike the majority of the Christian celebrations, which occur on set days, the Hindu festivities are based on the lunar calendar and so vary from year to year.

POP, BEAT & JAZZ MUSIC FESTIVAL
Date varies, between February and May
A two-day music fest at Panaji's swish Kala Academy.
Ⓦ www.kalaacademy.org Ⓔ kalaacademy@kalaacademy.org

SHIGMOTSAV
February to March
One of the main Hindu festivals, Shigmo, as it's also known, celebrates the end of winter. Running for a couple of weeks, it involves parades of

🔺 *Traditional dancers enliven festivals*

LIFESTYLE

floats in Panaji, Margao, Mapusa, Vasco da Gama and Ponda, folk dancing, and young people covering each other – and sometimes you – in brightly coloured flour and water.

CARNIVAL
Before Lent

Originally instituted by the Portuguese to celebrate the start of spring, Carnival has now widened its reach and welcomes people of every faith; many non-Goans also make the trip to attend. The revelry gets under way when the rotund character 'King Momo' decrees that everybody should have a good time. Celebrations include a colourful parade of floats, dancing, drinking, eating and general merrymaking. Carnival is one of the state's most popular festivals and if you fancy seeing it you need to book ahead.

PROCESSION OF ALL SAINTS
Fifth Monday of Lent

Starting from the Church of St Andrew, worshippers lug 30-plus statues on their shoulders around Old Goa and its neighbouring towns in the only event of this type to be held outside Rome. The piety of the day's procession gives way to more relaxed family fun in the evening.

BEACH BONANZA
From mid-April

Goans don't need religion as an excuse for a party. Beach Bonanza, which takes place on Sundays in Colva, is about nothing more than showing tourists a good time, with plenty of entertainment, drinking and dancing. The main action has now shifted from the beach to the village football ground.

◗ *Postboxes are clearly marked*

PRACTICAL INFORMATION
Tips & advice

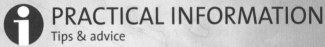

Accommodation

Price ratings are based on the average cost of a double room for one night.

£ under £50   **££** £50–£100   **£££** over £100

ANJUNA

Villa Anjuna £ Close to the beach and only a short walk from party zones, flea market and eateries, this hotel is modern and well run. Facilities include 24-hour coffee shop, and pool, Internet and Wi-Fi areas. ❸ Near Anjuna beachfront ❶ 0832 227 3443 Ⓦ www.anjunavilla.com

ARAMBOL

Famafa Beach Resort £ This cheap and cheerful hotel with 25 rooms makes a comfortable base to explore the area. All rooms have a balcony. ❸ Beach Road, Khalchawada ❶ 0832 224 2516 ❸ famafa-in@yahoo.com

ASVEM

Montego Bay Beach Village ££ Situated just off the beach, this sprawling and laid-back resort, full of Bedouin-style luxury tents and log cabins, is a cut above the rest. All tents have attached bathrooms and complete power supply. The resort restaurant is recommended. ❸ Vithaldas Waddo ❶ 98 22 150847 Ⓦ www.montegobaygoa.com

Yab Yum ££ Taking the trend for tents a little further, Yab Yum Beach Resort offers eco-friendly luxury 'pod' accommodation – made from all-local materials – that's half space-age, half coconut shell. The emphasis is on peace and relaxation; there's no TV, no music and no air-conditioning. On-site yoga is available and David, the in-house masseur, is very, very good. ❸ Asvem Beach Ⓦ www.yabyumresorts.com/en

BAGA

Colonia Santa Maria ££ Simple village-style complex of 100 rooms bang on Baga beach in the area called 'Baywatch'. Great location for

bars and shops with beach activity right on the doorstep, while the hotel restaurants and bar provide great nights in. ⓐ Baga Beach, Cobravaddo ⓣ 0832 665 7000 ⓦ www.csmgoa.com

BENAULIM

Park Hyatt £££ No expense or luxury spared at this top-notch palace set in spacious grounds. Facilities include the biggest spa in Goa, fine dining and a host of water activities on the sparkling beach. ⓐ Arossim Beach, Cansaulim ⓣ 0832 272 1234 ⓦ www.parkhyatt.com

CALANGUTE

Kerkar Retreat ££ A short walk from the beach, this smart boutique hotel of just five well-furnished rooms reflects the owner's taste in Goan furniture and Portuguese-style architecture. ⓐ Gaura Vaddo ⓣ 0832 227 6017 ⓦ www.subodhkerkar.com ⓔ subodhkerkar@satyam.net.in

CANDOLIM

Pretty Petal Guest House £ This spotlessly clean family-run guesthouse has 15 comfortable rooms with balcony or terrace and is only a short walk from the beach. ⓐ Camotim Waddo ⓣ 0832 248 9184 ⓦ www.prettypetalsgoa.com ⓔ prettypetalsgoa@indiatimes.com

PALOLEM

Café del Mar and Café del Sol £ Go for full party vibe at this stylish hut and bungalow complex. The Café del Mar bar next door provides round-the-clock entertainment. ⓐ Palolem Beach Road ⓣ 98 23 276520/98 23 313983 ⓦ www.cafedelmarpalolem.com

PANAJI

Panjim Inn ££ Impressive accommodation of 24 bedrooms in three 19th-century town houses near Ourem Creek. Period furniture and four-poster beds blend seamlessly with modern facilities such as cable TV, air conditioning and spacious bathrooms. ⓐ E-212, 31 Janeiro Road, Fontainhas ⓣ 0832 222 6523 ⓦ www.panjiminn.com

Preparing to go

GETTING THERE

By air

Current aviation regulations mean that if you take a scheduled flight from the UK and Europe to Goa you'll have to change planes, usually in Mumbai (Bombay), and sometimes in Delhi, or Colombo in Sri Lanka. Several major airlines, including BA, SWISS, Austrian Airlines, Air France, Emirates and Sri Lankan Airlines, link up with Jet Airways or Kingfisher to run flights from Europe with a stopover; Jet also operates out of London. From time to time airlines do offer discounts, but a scheduled flight is likely to set you back up to £500 in the high season.

A cheaper option can be to go on a charter flight, either with or without accommodation included, which also has the benefit of being direct, currently from Gatwick, Manchester and Birmingham. You should be able to get something for around £400, with further savings available if you book very far in advance or (sometimes) at the last minute. The law states that, whether you choose to come via a scheduled or charter flight, you must leave the same way. The journey time is around 11 hours.

If you're travelling from Ireland, you're likely to have to go via the UK. The US has direct flights to Mumbai, but it can be cheaper to come via Europe. Canadians can go via the US, Europe or Asia. From Australia, only Qantas flies non-stop to India, and leaving from New Zealand you will probably have a stopover in Asia.

Many people are aware that air travel emits CO_2, which contributes to climate change. You may be interested in the possibility of lessening the environmental impact of your flight through the charity **Climate Care**, which offsets your CO_2 by funding environmental projects around the world. Visit Ⓦ www.jpmorganclimatecare.com

By land

Driving to Goa from elsewhere in India is not recommended unless you're familiar with the conditions and have nerves of steel. Nor is hiring a car particularly cheap. But taxis and auto-rickshaw or tuk-tuk drivers

are often prepared to make long journeys from one town to another, and cheap public trains and buses from nearby cities and states are also an option. In the case of buses, you are likely to have to pay a bit more for a ticket on a private bus, which will be more comfortable and probably air-conditioned.

TOURISM AUTHORITY

India has been keenly plugging itself as a tourist destination lately under the 'Incredible India' slogan and has plenty of tourist offices around the world, including in London, Milan, Frankfurt, Paris, Amsterdam, New York, Los Angeles, Toronto, Sydney and Johannesburg. The full list of contact details is available at Ⓦ www.incredibleindia.org

It's also worth taking a look at the Goa Tourist Department's site. If you have a specific question you can also give them a call.
Ⓣ 0832 2438750/51/52 Ⓦ www.goa-tourism.org

BEFORE YOU LEAVE

Doctors recommend that you are up to date with your hepatitis A, polio, typhoid, tetanus-diphtheria and MMR jabs for all travel to India. Inoculation against yellow fever is required if you've recently visited an infected area. Depending on the circumstances of your trip – whether you're visiting rural areas, interacting closely with local people or coming into contact with animals – rabies, hepatitis B and Japanese encephalitis injections may also be necessary. Anti-malarial medication is strongly

TRAVEL INSURANCE

Taking out travel insurance is strongly recommended and inexpensive. The most basic packages start from around £1 a day for a two-week or month-long break. For three months, expect to pay around £80. However, essential-cover-only packages exclude certain activities and, if you intend to ride a motorbike, scuba-dive or similar, you may need to pay a bit more.

recommended. Consult your doctor at least a month before you go to ensure you have proper protection.

You should be able to buy pretty much anything you run out of on the trip. However, it can be worth taking a first-aid kit plus any medication with you.

ENTRY FORMALITIES

All foreign visitors to India require a visa and a passport valid for at least six months from your departure date. You can apply for a tourist visa in person or by post from the nearest Indian embassy, high commission or consulate general; the form is available online or you can pick one up in person. Unless there are any unusual circumstances – if you have dual nationality or are applying from outside your country of residence, for example – the procedure is fairly simple and shouldn't take much longer than a week. The fee is currently £30 for British nationals, and varies slightly from country to country. More information is available at
Ⓦ www.hcilondon.in

You're permitted by customs law to bring in a maximum of 200 cigarettes (or 50 cigars or 250 g/9 oz of loose tobacco), a litre of spirits and 250 ml (8½ fl oz) of perfume. Expensive items, for example electronic goods such as video cameras, technically ought to be declared on a Tourist Baggage Re-Export form, or you risk being charged duty on them when you leave India.

MONEY

The Indian currency is the rupee. In the main tourist resorts, banks, ATMs and bureaux de change are easy to find, and accept pounds, euros and dollars. Your hotel may also change your money for you, but it's wise to check the rate first.

Don't rely on your credit card outside Panaji – while some upmarket hotels and shops may take cards, the majority of low-budget hotels, restaurants and cafés don't. It's worth planning ahead with your money if you're going off the beaten track. Try not to accept torn banknotes as you may have trouble getting rid of them.

Mumbai was the victim of a serious terrorist attack in November 2008. If travelling to Goa via Mumbai check out the latest security situation with your travel agent or visit the UK Foreign and Commonwealth Office website on www.fco.gov.uk

CLIMATE

Goa's temperature stays hot throughout the year, averaging from 25 to 30°C (around 77 to 86°F). The holiday season runs roughly from October to March, with peak visiting time the two weeks over Christmas and New Year. This is a great time to visit for the party atmosphere, but you will pay for the privilege with higher prices and low availability. At either end of the season you can find great discounts and privacy, but you'll really feel the humidity in April and May, and by June the four-month monsoon season is kicking in, bringing heavy rains and rough seas. Few tourists choose to come at this time.

BAGGAGE ALLOWANCE

Baggage restrictions vary from one airline to another and, in the current political climate, from one month to the next. There's no substitute for checking your airline or operator's website in advance, giving them a call or checking with your travel agent. As a rule, scheduled airlines usually offer higher baggage allowances than chartered.

During your stay

AIRPORTS

Dabolim airport, the state's only one, is near Vasco da Gama and around 30 km (19 miles) from the capital Panaji. There's a prepaid taxi booth just outside, which displays the costs to certain destinations. You'll be besieged by taxi drivers as soon as you emerge. You should be able to bargain one down to a decent fare. Otherwise, turn left when you leave the airport and walk up the hill, where you can pick up buses to Vasco da Gama and continue your journey via another bus or on the train.

Bear in mind that the airport can be bureaucratic and chaotic, so on your way home it can be worth turning up more than the suggested two hours in advance.

☎ 0832 254 0795 🖷 0832 254 1863

COMMUNICATIONS

There are plenty of places from which you can make phone calls: look for the signs that read STD/ISD/PCO in small shops and kiosks. Some have coin-operated payphones; at others the call is metered and you pay at the end. Expect to pay up to 20 rupees a minute. Internet cafés are increasingly offering phone calls, which can work out a lot cheaper. There's good mobile reception in most areas. If you're staying for a while, you could buy a local SIM card (you'll need your passport).

Goa's postal service is reliable but slow, with letters sent overseas taking anything up to three weeks to arrive. You should pay less than 10 rupees to send a postcard abroad, while a letter may cost about double that. As well as at post offices, stamps are sometimes on sale along with postcards. Some hotels will also mail cards for you.

Postboxes are rectangular and red, and fairly easy to spot.

CUSTOMS

Watch out for the Indian side-to-side head movement in response to questions. Whether this means 'yes', 'no', 'maybe' or 'I don't know'

depends on the circumstances. If you need to extract crucial information, try to get a verbal answer.

DRESS CODES

While Goa is laid-back and fully geared up for tourists, it's still part of a very traditional country. Topless and nude sunbathing are against the law; while that is unlikely to be enforced, stripping off can still offend local sensibilities. Some restraint is appreciated. If you do decide to bare all, the hippy beaches of Anjuna, Arambol and relaxed Vagator are probably the best places to go to.

In religious buildings, modest dress is required. If you're visiting a temple, you should take off your shoes at the entrance, and it's good manners to offer to do so if going into an Indian person's home, although they may well tell you not to bother.

TELEPHONING GOA
From Europe 00 + 91 + 832 + number
From the US & Canada 011 + 91 + 832 + number
From Australia 0011 + 91 + 832 + number
From New Zealand 00 + 91 + 832 + number
From South Africa 00 + 91 + 832 + number

TELEPHONING ABROAD
UK 00 + 44 + number
US & Canada 00 + 1 + number
Australia 00 + 61 + number
New Zealand 00 + 64 + number
South Africa 00 + 27 + number

To get a telephone number, dial 191 or 197 for Directory Enquiries. 195 is the number for assistance with numbers that have changed. To get the operator, call 199.

ELECTRICITY

Goa's current is 230 to 240 volts/50 Hz. The plug socket is three round pins, but comes in two sizes. European appliances usually fit loosely into the smaller kind, but you may need to wedge the plug in place. Cheap adaptors are easy to find. Note that power cuts are common.

EMERGENCIES

Medical facilities in Goa may seem on the basic side to the Western patient. The best ones are based in the larger towns; fortunately, given the size of the state, you should never be too far away from somewhere with decent amenities. If you need medical treatment, the best thing is to ask for advice at your hotel; many of the hotels have a doctor on call and, even if they don't, they are likely to be able to point you in the right direction. Almost all doctors in Goa speak English. If you're out, a taxi driver should know the nearest place. In an emergency, bear in mind that calling an ambulance can be slow and your best bet may be to take a taxi instead.

EMERGENCY NUMBERS
Ambulance 102
Fire 101
Police 100
Tourist Police 0832 246 4260/0832 228 1328/0832 227 4031
Coastguard 1718

Apollo Victor Hospital ⓐ Malbhat, Margao ❶ 0832 272 8888
Ⓦ www.apollovictorhospital.com Ⓔ avhgoa@bsnl.in
Goa Medical College ⓐ Dayanand Bandodkar Marg ❶ 0832 245 8700
Goa Medical College Hospital ⓐ Bambolim, NH 17, 9 km (5¹/₂ miles) south of Panaji ❶ 0832 245 8700, 0832 223 3700 ❶ 0832 245 8727
Ⓔ goamed@hotmail.com
Mapusa Clinic ⓐ Mapusa Clinic Road, Mapusa ❶ 0832 226 3343

There are no embassies in Goa itself.

Australia High Commission 🏢 3rd Floor, 36 Maker Chambers VI, 220 Nariman Point, Mumbai 📞 022 6669 2000 🌐 www.india.embassy.gov.au

British Deputy High Commission 🏢 Maker Chambers IV, 2nd Floor, 222 Jamnalal Bajaj Road, Nariman Point, Mumbai 📞 022 6650 2222 ✉ consular.bombay@fco.gov.uk

British Tourist Assistance Office in Goa 🏢 S-13/14 Dempo Towers, Patto Plaza, Panaji 📞 0832 243 8897 ✉ assistance@goaukconsular.org

Irish Embassy 🏢 230 Jor Bagh, New Delhi 3 📞 011 2462 6733 📠 011 2469 7053 🌐 www.irelandinindia.com

New Zealand High Commission 🏢 Sir Edmund Hillary Marg, Chanakyapuri, New Delhi 📞 011 2688 3170 📠 011 2688 3165 🌐 www.nzembassy.com

South African High Commission 🏢 B-18, Vasant Marg, New Delhi 📞 011 2614 9411 ✉ highcommissioner@sahc_india.com

US Consulate General 🏢 Lincoln House, 78 Bhulabhai Desai Road, Mumbai 📞 022 2363 3611 🌐 http://mumbai.usconsulate.gov

The 24-hour helpline 📞 0832 2412121 has information on everything from medical care to restaurants.

GETTING AROUND

Car hire

Because of India's chaotic driving conditions, few tourists opt to hire a car. It's usually much easier and cheaper to get the car with the driver, which can be done either through a travel agent or hotel, or just by negotiating with a taxi driver. A day's worth of travelling shouldn't set you back any more than 1,000 rupees. If you're not coming back to the starting point, clarify whether the driver's return journey is included.

If you do intend to drive yourself, it's a good idea to bring an international licence with you. Traffic in the cities can be a nightmare of hold-ups and hooting. In the country, roads are usually uneven and there aren't many signs or streetlights.

In India, as in Britain, you drive on the left.

Motorbike & bicycle hire

A motorbike is perfect for zipping around to remote beaches. You can hire anything from a scooter up to an Enfield. This can be done through your hotel, a travel agent or on the street. Although few tourists seem to bother, wearing a helmet is required by law and is also a good idea, given India's appalling road-safety statistics. If you're not going that far, renting a bicycle (or even buying one, if you're staying a while) is another option.

Public transport

Taking a bus in Goa is not only ridiculously cheap, but also a fun way to see some of the local life. Buses don't tend to go along the coast; you'll probably need to come inland and change. The main hubs are Mapusa, Panaji and Margao. You normally pay the conductor on board. Some private buses offer more comfort for a higher fare.

The state has two main railway lines, one running north–south and the other east–west. Few of the stations are well placed for the beach resorts, though. Train enquiry line (Margao Station): ☎ 0832 271 2790.

HEALTH, SAFETY & CRIME

As in the rest of India, take care with what you eat and drink. Mindful of the importance of their reputations, the vast majority of Goa's hotels, restaurants and beach shacks maintain high standards of hygiene and use bottled water for ice. Check the seals on bottled water to ensure they have not been refilled with tap water. Healthcare in Goa is not expensive, but the standards are lower than you might be used to. The most reliable hospitals are listed in the Emergencies section.

Goa generally feels safe, but the preponderance of 'rich' tourists in a very poor country does have its inherent risks. Violent crimes, such as muggings, are unusual but do occur. Take care to secure your possessions, whether they are in the hotel, on your person or on the beach while you're swimming. Be discreet with your valuables, and pay close attention in crowded places. Women travellers in particular should avoid walking alone at night in quiet areas. Be particularly wary about accepting food or drink from strangers, as drugging incidents, though

rare, have been reported. Anything involving export licences or money changing should set your alarm bells ringing.

You may encounter a few low-level hassles, such as taxi drivers who want to take you to shops or hotels that give them commission, but these can usually be dealt with by a firm refusal.

MEDIA

It's easy to find English media in Goa. There are four English-language newspapers, *The Navhind Times*, *The Herald*, *The Times of India* and *The Gomantak Times*, plus the weekly *Goan Observer* and monthly magazine *Goa Today*. Your hotel is likely to have the usual selection of cable channels – BBC World, CNN, MTV, HBO, the Discovery Channel and so on. Some local Indian channels, both television and radio, also broadcast in English.

OPENING HOURS

Many shops catering to tourists start the day early and stay open as long as holidaymakers are up and about. Most restaurants and beach shacks open around 07.00 or 08.00 and serve food until at least 23.00, sometimes later. Banks tend to operate from 10.00 to 14.00 from Monday to Friday, and from 10.00 to 12.00 on Saturday, although some stay open later, especially in larger towns. Bureaux de change often stay open until the early evening or later. Religious buildings keep differing hours, but temples frequently open from very early in the morning. Businesses often close for a siesta, from 12.00 or 13.00 to 15.00 or 15.30.

RELIGION

Almost two-thirds of Goans are Hindu and around one-third Christian – a legacy of Portuguese rule; a minority are Muslim. Goans are generally tolerant of other people's faiths.

TIME DIFFERENCES

Goa is $5^{1}/_{2}$ hours ahead of GMT, $4^{1}/_{2}$ ahead of most of mainland Europe. It is $10^{1}/_{2}$ ahead of Eastern Standard Time and $13^{1}/_{2}$ ahead of Pacific Standard Time, $5^{1}/_{2}$ hours behind Sydney and $7^{1}/_{2}$ behind Auckland.

TIPPING

It's customary to tip in restaurants and in your hotel. Tipping 10 per cent of your bill when eating out is the norm; in hotels 10 or 20 rupees should suffice. There's no need to tip a taxi driver who takes you a short distance, but if you've hired the driver for the day he will probably expect a little extra.

TOILETS

The majority of conveniences you encounter will be Western style. All restaurants and beach shacks have their own toilets or access to one, which are usually clean enough. It's best to carry around some tissues as an emergency loo-roll stash; Indians don't use toilet paper.

TRAVELLERS WITH DISABILITIES

Goa is not the easiest place to get around if you have impaired mobility. The pavements – where there are any – can be narrow and uneven, and few facilities outside the top hotels have wheelchair access. But Goans are usually helpful and accommodating where they can be, and the low costs mean that staying in adapted accommodation and travelling with a car and a driver should be affordable.

The following organisations offer various degrees of advice to travellers with disabilities:

Disability Goa ⓐ Star Investments, Opp. Head Post Office, Panaji, Goa
❶ 0832 242 7160 ⓦ www.disabilitygoa.com ⓔ dragoa@rediffmail.com
The Royal Association for Disability and Rehabilitation does not offer an advice service for individuals, but its website has a news bulletin board on which the editor posts details of overseas travel services. ⓐ 12 City Forum, 250 City Road, London EC1V 8AF ❶ 020 7250 3222
ⓦ www.radar.org.uk ⓔ radar@radar.org.uk
Tourism for All ⓐ c/o Vitalise, Shap Road Industrial Estate, Shap Road, Kendal, Cumbria LA9 6NZ ❶ 0845 124 9971 ❶ 01539 735 567
ⓦ www.tourismforall.org.uk

A

accommodation 112–13
air travel 114, 118
Anjuna 25–9
Arambol 14–19
architecture 53, 76, 83
art galleries
    Bom Jesus Basilica Art Gallery
        83–4
    Kerkar Art Complex 39
    Kristu Kala Mandir Art Gallery 85
Art Park Campal 54
Asvem 48–51
Ayurveda 39, 62, 71–2, 108

B

Baga 31–5
baggage allowance 117
Bardez taluka 76–7
beaches 14, 20–21, 25, 31, 37–9, 44,
    48–9, 53–4, 61–2, 66, 70–71,
    107–8
Benaulim 66–9
birdwatching 81–2
boats 40–41, 46, 48–9, 53, 68, 78, 81,
    107
buses 83, 115, 122

C

Calangute 37–43
Candolim 44–7
casino 59
cathedral 86
children 105–6
churches
    Basilica of Bom Jesus 83–4
    Church of Our Lady of the
        Immaculate Conception 54
    Church of Our Lady of Mercy 62
    Church of St Francis of Assisi 84
climate 117
Colva 61–5
communications 118
consulates 121

crime 122–3
customs and duty 116

D

disabilities, travellers with 124
dolphin-watching 61–2, 68
Dona Paula Beach 53
Dr Salim Ali Bird Sanctuary
    81–2
dress 119
driving 114, 121

E

electricity 120
elephants 106
embassies and consulates 121
emergencies 120–21
etiquette 106, 119
excursions 40–41, 46, 55–6, 76–94

F

family 105–6
ferries 81
festivals 109–10
fishing 61
food and drink 96–101
    fruit 97–8
    menu decoder 100–101
    places to eat 16–19, 21–3, 27–9,
        33–5, 41–3, 44, 46–7, 51, 57–9,
        62, 64–5, 69, 72–4, 77, 80, 82,
        86, 89, 93–4, 99
    rice 97
    seafood 69, 93, 96
    tea 98
Fort Aguada 78–80

G

gardens 54, 93

H

health 115–16, 122
hippies 8, 14, 25
hospitals 120

I

insurance 115

K

Kala Academy 59

M

Mandovi River 53
Mandrem 48–51
Margao 91–4
massage 108
media 123
meditation 16, 45
Miramar 53
money 116
Morjim 48–51
motorbikes 122
Municipal Gardens 93
museums
    Archaeology Museum 83
    Goa State Museum 54
    Houses of Goa Museum 76

N

nightlife 18–19, 22–3, 28–9, 31, 33–5,
    41–3, 46–7, 51, 57–9, 62, 64–5, 69,
    72–4, 77, 94

O

Old Goa 83–6
opening hours 123

P

Palolem 70–74
Panaji 53–9
passports and visas 116
phones 118, 119
Ponda 87–9
post 118

R

religion 109–10, 123

S

safety 122–3
scuba diving 33
shopping 61, 66–7, 102–4
    bargaining 103–4
    food and drink 93
    markets 20, 25–6, 33, 39, 66, 91,
        93, 102–3
    souvenirs 26, 104
    textiles 104
Sinquerim 78–80
smoking 99
spice farms 87
swimming 53–4

T

Tai Chi 16
taxis 104, 120, 121
temples 87, 89
    Damodar Temple 93
    Maruti Temple 54–5
    Shantadurga Temple 89
    Shri Mahalsa 89
    Sri Manguesh Temple 89
time differences 123
tipping 124
toilets 124
tourist information 115, 121, 124
trains 122
TV 123

V

Vagator 20–23

W

watersports 14–16, 31, 33, 40, 53–4,
    61–2, 68, 70, 107–8
wildlife sanctuaries 81–2, 106

Y

yoga 16, 26–7, 39, 45, 49, 71–2, 108

ACKNOWLEDGEMENTS

Thomas Cook Publishing wishes to thank VASILE SZAKACS, to whom the copyright belongs, for the photographs in this book, except for the following images:

Matthew Parker pages 5, 10–11, 23, 28, 42, 49, 50, 97
World Pictures/Photoshot pages 13, 15, 21, 26, 27, 32, 38, 45, 63, 65, 68, 71, 77, 79, 82, 92, 95, 105

For CAMBRIDGE PUBLISHING MANAGEMENT LIMITED:
Project editor: Ed Robinson
Layout: Paul Queripel
Proofreaders: Cath Senker & Jan McCann

Send your thoughts to
books@thomascook.com

- Found a beach bar, peaceful stretch of sand or must-see sight that we don't feature?

- Like to tip us off about any information that needs a little updating?

- Want to tell us what you love about this handy little guidebook and, more importantly, how we can make it even handier?

Then here's your chance to tell all! Send us ideas, discoveries and recommendations today and then look out for your valuable input in the next edition of this title.

Email to the above address or write to:
pocket guides Series Editor, Thomas Cook Publishing, PO Box 227, Unit 9, Coningsby Road, Peterborough PE3 8SB, UK.